THE ~~WORK~~
OF THE
ASSOCIATE
PASTOR

ALAN R. RUDNICK

JUDSON PRESS
PUBLISHERS SINCE 1824

Join our mailing list for updates and special offers.
www.judsonpress.com/mailing_list.cfm

ACKNOWLEDGMENTS

First, I would like to thank my wife, Christine, who is a constant support of my ministry and a fathomless source of love. Without her support, none of my ministry and work would be possible. Second, thank you to all the senior and associate pastors who have ministered to me through the years. Special thanks to Rev. Charlie Updike, my mentor and friend, who is my consistent supporter and confidant. Last, I would like to express my sincere gratitude to Kristen Champion-Terrell for her help with my book.

THE WORK OF THE ASSOCIATE PASTOR
© 2012 by Judson Press, Valley Forge, PA 19482-0851
All rights reserved.

Judson Press has made every effort to trace the ownership of all quotes. In the event of a question arising from the use of a quote, we regret any error made and will be pleased to make the necessary correction in future printings and editions of this book.

Bible quotations marked NRSV are from the New Revised Standard Version Bible, copyright ©1989, Division of Christian Education of the National Council of the Churches of Christ in the United States of America. Used by permission. All rights reserved.

Library of Congress Cataloging-in-Publication Data
Rudnick, Alan R. The work of the associate pastor / Alan R. Rudnick. — 1st ed.
p. cm. Includes bibliographical references. ISBN 978-0-8170-1709-5 (pbk. :alk. paper) 1. Associate clergy. 2. Pastoral theology. I. Title. BV674.R83 2012
253 — dc23   2012023018

Printed in the U.S.A.
First Edition, 2012.

CONTENTS

INTRODUCTION

While I was an associate pastor, I was asked to give the invocation at the National Football League Players Gala in Washington, DC. During the gala, which was also a fundraiser for the Special Olympics, I was introduced to a variety of National Football League players, politicians, philanthropists, dignitaries, and celebrities. One of the players was gracious enough to allow me to take a picture with him. After I introduced myself as an associate pastor in a local congregation, the professional football player asked, "What does an associate pastor do anyway?"

Sometimes, congregations have the same question for their associate pastors because they do not understand or have not been properly introduced to the role of the associate pastor. Denominational leaders and church leaders have not adequately informed congregations about the role and nature of the associate pastorate.

When I finished seminary, I was searching for churches looking to hire an associate pastor. As I searched for associate pastor positions, I found that many congregations had difficulty articulating what they were looking for in an associate pastor. Most wanted a seminary graduate who was a biblically minded and Christ-centered individual. Apart from those qualifications, most churches seemed to be fumbling in the dark with questions that sought to match the strength of the candidate with the position. I felt as though churches were looking for a body to fill their vacant position instead of finding an individual who was ready to answer God's call to the associate pastorate.

I began to be frustrated with the apparent lack of focus the committees put into the discernment process of calling an associate pastor. Some even wanted to fill the associate position based on the cheapest request for a compensation package instead of on a process of focused prayer and spiritual discernment. I found myself wishing that committee members and church leaders had a resource to draw upon for this important task of calling an associate pastor. It is my hope and prayer that this work will enable churches, denominational leaders, and lay people to grasp the salient nuances that go into calling an associate pastor.

Even during my preparation for ministry, I found that my seminary experience did not emphasize the role of the associate pastor. That personal experience has been echoed in conversations with seminary graduates around the country. It appears that seminaries are not equipping graduates with the education that is required to understand the role of an associate pastor. Most seminaries seek to produce solo pastors who are biblically, theologically, and spiritually prepared to take on ministry settings in congregations. The seminaries that I studied have little to no course work geared toward developing and training associate pastors. Seminaries train youth pastors, children's pastors, music pastors, or counseling pastors, but almost none of the course work involves examining the identity of the associate within the congregation or how the associate functions as a specialized minister. Associate pastor responsibilities can encompass those roles but the associate is usually ordained, college- or seminary-educated, and a spiritually called ministry professional.

This book is by no means an exhaustive survey of associate pastor work but is a resource that will enable pastors, congregants, lay leaders, and church staff to understand the work of the associate pastor better, thereby equipping churches with the necessary knowledge to encourage associates in their ministry. When associate pastors feel and know their work is appreciated and supported, churches can have flourishing ministries that reach people for Christ.

The work of associate pastor is a great way for seminarians and ministry-minded individuals to get their feet wet in church ministry. Supportive ministry positions are crucial to the work of the church, but often congregants and even clergy are confused about how an associate pastor should function within the church. There are limited resources to guide congregations to finding, choosing, and supporting associate pastors in their work.

The goal of this work is to provide insight and reflection upon the ministry specialty of associate pastoring. For the associate pastor, numerous challenges arise from being what has been called the "second chair" in a church setting. In a symphony orchestra, the "second chair" is usually an individual who is gifted in musical ability but follows the lead of the more talented first chair. The analogy of second chair has served as the primary model for understanding associate work in coordination with the senior or head pastor.

This book will seek to go beyond the analogy of the second chair to provide both a biblical understanding and a family systems-based approach to the associate pastorate. The paradigm of the second chair relies heavily upon a power-oriented understanding, whereas this book will seek to view the associate as equally important but distinctively different. Viewing associates as second best or as underlings has produced many frustrated, bitter, and burned-out clergy. Drawing from case studies, this book will provide a real-world view of this specialized ministry. These case studies come from my experiences and from experiences shared by colleagues and friends who have participated in a range of associate pastorates from the fruitful to the challenging. It is my hope that these experiences will help ministers, search committees, pastoral relations committees, seminarians, lay people, and senior pastors to work better with associate pastors.

Often, it is believed that associate pastors are ministers who are "paying the rent" to become senior or lead pastors. This is far from the truth. If associate pastors and congregations believe this premise, then everyone involved will have a difficult time understanding the true role of associate work. Associate work is not about using the church as a stepping stone to the next ministry. Rather, the fundamental role of associate pastors is *to support the vision of the church through their gifts and calling to enable the church to accomplish its goals.*

That fundamental role being stated, it should also be noted that associate work does provide helpful and valuable ministry opportunities to learn and grow should God ultimately lead the associate into a senior or solo pastorate. However, numerous associate pastors who serve in the areas of Christian education, music, children and youth work, and counseling have been ministering in their specialty for decades; they are both successful and established in their primary calling. These associates have no desire to leave their specialized fields for a senior or solo position. When associate pastors do become senior pastors, it is often because their calling has changed (as callings do) or because they sense that they are ready to move into leadership in a multi-staff environment.

As a child and a youth, I was indelibly impressed by a variety of associate pastors who demonstrated how important associate pastors are to the people and to the church as a whole. My youth pastors introduced me to Christ as Lord and Savior and made my church experience fun, exciting, and dynamic. My music pastors taught me the beauty of hymns, songs, and anthems, as well as their biblical and theological significance. My Christian education pastors made sure that my Sunday school teachers were well-trained and educated in teaching Scripture. All of these pastors, under the direction of the senior pastor, enabled me to deepen my faith and to discover my call to the pastoral ministry. Moreover, as a result of the collaborative pastoral leadership at my home church, we grew from a small family church to a thriving congregation with hundreds of members.

My story is just a small voice among advocates of associate pastors in the life of the parish, and it represents a fruitful outcome of associate work. Once I became an associate pastor, I saw the position of the associate from both the pew and the pulpit. This perspective grounded me as a pastoral leader to focus my ministry in love of Christ and the love of the people.

Throughout these chapters, the reader will find that successful associate pastorates stem from congregations and associate pastors who clearly articulate their desires and what they feel God is calling each to do in the life of the church. Open and honest communication and trust between the associate pastor and congregation is the cornerstone of a healthy church. In addition, healthy communication between the associate and the senior pastor is critical to the success of longer pastorates. More than half (53%) of associate pastors report that pastoral staff conflicts led to their departure from the ministry of the local church.[1] Conflicts among church staff often arise from unclear guidelines, boundaries, and responsibilities for associate pastors.

It is my hope that this book will help decrease such conflict by clarifying the nature of associate work within the shared life of the church. Indeed, understanding the vision of associate work is essential. As the pithy proverb states, "Without vision, the people fail." If no one understands the vision of associate work, the people will not come to understand what the associate pastor has to offer through specialized or supportive ministry gifts. This book seeks to provide that vision and clarification through reflection on real-life situations of how associate pastors succeed and fail.

Whether the reader is an associate pastor, a senior pastor, a seminarian, or a member of the church staff or pastoral relations committee, I pray that you will benefit from this work as a guide. One of the greatest gifts that we have is education. Such education will enable associates to work better with pastors, leaders, lay people, congregations as a whole, and other staff.

Understanding the nature and role of the associate pastor must be at the forefront of the congregation's agenda any time an associate is hired.

NOTES
1. Dean R. Hoge and Jacqueline E. Wenger, *Pastors in Transition: Why Clergy Leave Local Church Ministry* (Grand Rapids: Eerdmans, 2005), 80.

PART ONE

The Work of the Associate Pastor

CHAPTER 1

What Is an Associate Pastor?

When I was in high school, my counselor sat down with me to discuss the obligatory "What do you want to do when you grow up?" questionnaire. I completed the questionnaire, and I scored high in the categories of teacher, social worker, and counselor, but nothing on the questionnaire noted clergy, much less the position of associate pastor. I knew I wanted to start ministry as an associate pastor, but I did not know what form that ministry would take. And even as I filled out the questionnaire, I thought about how many people have benefited from associate pastors but how that vocation is almost never identified in our culture on surveys, lists, or job preparation material.

For that reason, we begin with the question, "What is an associate pastor?" At the basic level, the associate pastor is what any other pastor is: a servant leader.

Bishop William Willimon appropriately identifies the origin of this model: "Pastors take Jesus as a model for their ministry. . . . Servant is the name Jesus gave to himself and his work on our behalf."[1] Christ is the model for all pastors: senior pastors, youth pastors, music pastors, education pastors, children's pastors, and all types of associate pastors.

All pastors must be servants, but the associate pastor, by the nature of the position, is charged with serving, supporting, and equipping God's people and to do so under the direction of the senior pastor. To narrow down the role of the associate pastor is to see the associate as someone who holds membership in Christ's body and who is set apart by the act of ordination or license to share the gospel, to assist in shepherding a congregation, and to draw the people into community, most often through a specialized ministry. The work of the associate pastor is a secondary role in the leadership of the church, but by no means is the associate any less important than the senior or lead pastor.

A misconception exists that associate pastors are not needed because churches in many areas of the country are not growing enough to be able to support an associate pastor. This could not be further than the truth. In 2006, a Hartford Institute for Religion Research and the Leadership Network published a study that found that congregations drawing 2,000 or more in total attendance doubled that attendance from 2001–2005.[2] With an increase in church attendance and membership, a congregation typically increases its staff by adding specialty ministers and associate pastors. In this study, these large or megachurches averaged twenty full-time leadership staff (pastoral ministry positions) under the senior pastor.[3] And while many observers have commented that only nondenominational churches are growing, this study noted that 60 to 65 percent of larger churches are denominational, thus dispelling the myth of growth only among nondenominational churches.[4]

Especially in larger churches, associate pastors often form the backbone of the staff because they are often the ones who drive the ministries and programs of the church, including successful music, small-group, youth, children's, and education ministries. On the basis of the Hartford Institute study, it is possible to conclude that associate pastors are needed more than ever to meet the growing demands of church ministry. Large churches are not the only ones that employ an associate pastor. Small and medium-sized churches often rely on part-time and full-time ministers to assist in the ministries of their congregations. Generally, for every 100 people in attendance in a Sunday morning worship service, a church should have one associate pastor or professional program ministry staff member.

No matter what size your congregation is, you might carefully and prayerfully consider adding an associate pastor. Small and medium-sized churches often seek to discern whether or not the congregation is able financially to support an associate pastor. These churches worry about finding funding to support another minister. The effect on the church budget is not insignificant, of course. However, a variety of denominations, Christian-based charities, and nonprofits are willing to support congregations that incur the additional budgetary cost for associates by providing grants for several years until the church is able to support the associate pastor. Such charities include The Fund for Theological Education and the Lilly Foundation.

Associates in Scripture

Our scriptural guide for the role of an associate is found in both the Old and New Testaments. One of the strongest examples of the senior-associate relationship is that of Moses and Joshua. Joshua supported Moses' leadership by leading God's people into conflict with Amalek (Exodus 17) and accompanying Moses to Mount Sinai when Moses received the Ten Commandments (Exodus 34). In Numbers 14, Joshua was sent into the land of Canaan so that he could report back to Moses the status of the land. Joshua was such an effective secondary leader that he was later charged by God to take God's people to the Promised Land, something that Moses was not able to accomplish.

The relationship between Moses and Joshua was clear. In the New Revised Standard Version, the word *assistant* is used in Exodus 24:13, Exodus 33:11, Deuteronomy 1:38, and Numbers 11:28. Ultimately Joshua's experiences as Moses' assistant equipped the younger man to learn what it takes to become an anointed leader of God's people.

4

In the New Testament, the shared ministry of Paul and Timothy is often referred to as an associate-senior pastor relationship. In Philippians 4:3 Paul writes about his fellow ministry leaders using the Greek word *suzugos*, which can be translated as "associate." Paul charges and encourages Timothy to "what you have heard from me through many witnesses entrust to faithful people who will be able to teach others as well" (2 Timothy 2:2). Timothy is receiving direction from his fellow worker in the ministry, but clearly he is receiving this direction from Paul as an associate would receive direction from a senior pastor.

Paul mentored Timothy, and in turn, Timothy mentored others to teach the gospel. Paul told Timothy to teach sound doctrine (1 Timothy 1:3-11; 2 Timothy 1:13) and to be an exemplar of this doctrine lived out (1 Timothy 4:6). Paul wanted Timothy to fulfill his definitive responsibility, which was to "guard what is entrusted to you" (1 Timothy 6:20).

Paul had other associates: Silas, John Mark, Priscilla, Aquila, and Apollos were selected to assist in his ministry. All had roles that were similar to those of an associate and a senior pastor. However, it is significant that in the beginning of his ministry, Paul served more as an assistant to Barnabas (Acts 13). If the great apostle to the Gentiles benefited from working with a seasoned minister, this is encouragement for contemporary associate pastors.

Attributes of the Associate Pastor

In general, five attributes will lead to a successful tenure as an associate pastor.

Be a Shepherd

First, the associate needs to be a shepherd. Christ often painted himself as the Good Shepherd. The motif of the pastor as shepherd is helpful. In the ancient world, sheep would keep close together at night, which was the time of greatest danger. The shepherd would keep close to the flock to guard them. This imagery provides an example of how pastors must gently guide congregations through good times and bad times. The shepherd walks beside the sheep and sometimes must encourage the sheep to go in the right direction. Pastors need to walk beside the people as servant leaders, not placing themselves above the people in terms of power or ego. Thomas Oden, in his classic book *Pastoral Theology*, lends a helpful insight to the model of pastors as shepherds:

> The vocation of the pastor: to know the parish territory, its dangers, its green meadows, its steep precipices, its seasons, and possibilities. The pastor leads the flock to spring water and safe vegetation. The flock recognize their own good through the shepherd's voice. They do not see it in their interest to follow strangers. They know their own shepherd will not mislead them. The shepherd is able to anticipate their needs in advance and is willing to deal with each one individually.[6]

The relationship of the shepherd and flock clearly illustrates the need for a loving individual to guide God's people through the Christian life. Shepherding comes only after years of prayer, observation, spiritual reflection, and the gift of a servant's heart. Matthew 9:36 states, "Then Jesus saw the crowds, and he had compassion for them because they were harassed and helpless, like a sheep without a shepherd." Just as Jesus had compassion for the crowds, so pastors must have compassion for others.

Associate pastors also put themselves under the guiding presence of Christ. In turn, associates must shepherd others who are Sunday school teachers, youth leaders, child educators, deacons, and caregivers. As clergy, associate pastors are meant to shepherd as the ancient shepherds loved their flock, which means being willing to surrender time to guide these lay leaders. Pastors, both associate and senior, are to lead by giving of self for the good of others. More importantly, clergy are to lead in a way that brings others to Christ and through Christ to our Father God in heaven. We see in the media that leaders are often self-promoting, self-loving, and self-centered. Being an associate also requires sacrificing self-interest and ego. This is in opposition to what the world demands of leaders.

Be a Team Player

Second, the associate pastor needs to be a team player. The senior or lead pastor, along with associates and other staff, work in mutual cooperation. This is vital to the health of a local congregation. For senior pastors, such mutuality means resisting any urge to micromanage other church staff and setting aside any insecurities or attitudes to cultivate an environment of trust and respect for all team members.

Associate pastors must also set aside ego, attitude, and insecurities in order to focus on the work at hand, which is to love and care for the congregation and the ministries of the church. Being a team player means knowing your role and knowing your area of ministry. Associate pastors need to accept their supportive role and have enough self-esteem to affirm that their role is significant in the life of the church.

Team participation means being a cheerleader for others. Encouraging church members, other leaders, and the church staff is a critical aspect of effective pastoral leadership—for senior and associate pastors alike. As a cheerleader, the pastor becomes someone who celebrates with others when they succeed, thereby building team relationships.

Associates and senior pastors also need to be cautious. The temptation is to drift into the dark side of leadership. The darker side of leadership can be understood as "the inner urges, compulsions, and dysfunctions of our personality that often go unexamined or remain unknown to us."[7] These inner shadows seek what we might call "secondary gain." Secondary gain occurs when an associate pastor builds up a youth group because it builds up his or her broken ego. Secondary gain might be the motive behind a senior pastor's arbitrary decision to cut the budget for a music program because the music pastor's popularity is a threat to the senior pastor's own. Secondary gain is harmful when we seek our own selfish needs, but it also places ourselves before God. Placing ourselves and our egos ahead of God's divine purpose creates an idol that we worship. The idol we create becomes the ministry we are leading or the position we hold, not for God's glory, but for our own. This dark side of leadership has negative consequences when people are hurt, relationships are broken, and trust is bankrupted.

Be Self-differentiated

Third, the associate pastor needs to be self-differentiated. Self-differentiation is defined as "the degree to which people are able to distinguish between the feeling process and the intellectual process."[8] It describes the clarity needed to recognize that the response someone may have to a pastoral decision is not necessarily a response to the pastor as an individual. In lay terms, we might say that the associate pastor needs to know when not to take things personally!

For example, how would you react as associate pastor responsible for music if a church member approached you after a worship service and mentioned that the last hymn was not her favorite because it was the hymn sung at her father's funeral? Would you be able to differentiate her candid comments from a personal critique of you or your ministry? "Painful memories come to my mind of watching my father die." You may feel guilty for picking the hymn, but intellectually you should not take responsibility for unknowingly picking a song that carries sad memories for a member of the congregation. The person who does not self-differentiate would likely feel insecure and defensive about the comment and perhaps take the comment as a personal attack against his or her ministry abilities.

Because the associate pastor serves both the congregation and the senior pastor, the need to self-differentiate is all the more critical. The ability to minimize anxiety about people, situations, or relationships is a key to healthy ministry. Also key to self-differentiation is a clear grasp of personal identity—strengths and vulnerabilities, expertise and gaps in knowledge, as well as emotional baggage that may be attached to such strengths and vulnerabilities. For example, if I take particular pride in my ministry specialty, does that mean I will be more or less receptive to constructive critique in that area? And if I already know I am weak in a specific skill set, will I be more or less open to suggestions for improvement? As clergy, associates will keep self in balance by knowing their own fears.

Self-differentiated pastors will also obtain balance in their personal and professional lives by not becoming entrenched emotionally and personally in conflict. Pastors must be able to compartmentalize negative feelings and thoughts when dealing with difficult situations. A self-differentiated individual sees the situation aside from any personal differences or personal grief. This includes knowledge of self, convictions that are sturdy and apparent, and an aptitude to stand firm when strained by others. The self-differentiated pastor must have clear boundaries. Establishing these boundaries will be defined in later chapters. In addition, projections of emotion from staff and congregants on to the associate pastor cannot be taken personally.

Be an Organizational Leader
Fourth, the associate pastor must be an organizational leader. Associate pastors must embody Christian leadership by becoming competent organizational leaders to support the senior pastor. That means actively participating in or initiating strategic planning, constructive evaluations, and collaborative motivation

of others who share in leading organizational structures. Although the senior pastor may be responsible for the overall organizational leadership of the church, associate pastors must be a visible and productive member of the church's leadership team. Using a baseball illustration, associates may lead off on the batting order or they may be asked to bat later in the lineup so that others can have opportunities. No matter how prominent an associate is in the organizational structure of a church, every associate benefits from opportunities to lead others.

Organizational leadership includes long-term thinking. Good pastoral leadership typically starts with a mission statement, moves toward clarification of roles, and culminates in a statement of goals. Using this model helps define the mission of church as well and helps create a focus. In turn, this type of organizational leadership creates a trickle-down effect to pastoral staff and lay people, including deacons, board members, teachers, and other members of the congregation.

In order to lead others to a goal, a leader must know how to obtain the goal. Planning how to get there is key. Some key strategies for an associate pastor to lead other people in their ministry area are through focusing on the future orientation of the church, enhancing optimism among the congregants, nurturing creativity and building on the assets and gifts of lay people, and responding to unmet needs. As a pastor of the pastoral team, an associate needs to create an atmosphere that moves toward the focus of the ministry. This means that empowerment of the church members to take ownership is critical in order for a ministry to grow. A ministry rooted in organization and leadership is necessary for a pastor to work and minister efficiently.

Be Authentic

Fifth, the associate pastor needs to be authentic. How do associates embody authenticity? By being real, which means everything they do and say must be genuine. Ministry is no place for putting on a face of perfectionism or adopting a holier-than-thou attitude. Most people can see through a facade of self-righteous actions and recognize a person who needs attention or hides unhealthy insecurities. While inauthentic ministers demand respect because of their title or their position alone, authentic pastors earn respect by striving to do the right thing in any and every situation. Authentic leaders are not interested in saving face or building up overinflated self-esteem. Rather, they follow the example of Jesus, who didn't claim the equality with God that was his by right but took on the role of a servant and met people where they were (see Philippians 2:1-11). Jesus sought to be on the same level of those to whom he ministered. No ego, power plays, or presuppositions interfered with ministry to those who sought wholeness.

By seeking to be authentic in service to the congregation, an associate will be perceived by members to be one who desires to serve out of faithfulness to God's Word. When people see the associate's willingness to serve, seeking the church's best and putting the congregation first, the church will learn to work well with the associate pastor. A positive attitude toward pastoral leaders translates into fruitful ministry wherein all people are seen as equals who are valued and cared for.

* * *

These five positive qualities—servant leadership, team spirit, self-differentiation, organizational leadership, and authenticity— lead associates to a world where they can become effective ministers by standing true to themselves and being faithful to God. Embodying these qualities is not an easy task, but it is a task that is achievable when an associate is truly called by God and not acting out of his or her own selfish needs. As Christian leaders, we all want to be successful. There is nothing wrong with that desire—the danger is in wanting to be so successful that we will do anything to achieve our goals. When leadership is approached instead from a positive and self-giving mindset, associate pastors grow into well-rounded ministers who are loved by the congregation and valued by colleagues in church leadership.

Discussion Questions for Churches

1. What are your needs as a church in terms of supportive or associate leaders?
2. How might your church benefit from an associate pastor?
3. What does the church body look for in an associate pastor?
4. How can your church leaders aid the associate pastor(s) in your church to embody the five qualities of an associate pastor?
5. What does your church staff need to work effectively with associate pastors?
6. To what extent does your church staff work as a team? What is needed to work better?
7. What is the best quality of your associate pastor(s)?
8. How do your pastoral leaders organize the ministries they are responsible for?

Discussion Questions for Associate Pastors

1. Why did you become an associate pastor?
2. Does your role follow the examples of associates or supportive leaders? Why or why not?
3. What are your best qualities as an associate pastor?
4. How do you embody the five qualities of an associate pastor?
5. How can you embody the notion of shepherd leadership for your church?
6. Are you a team player within your congregation? Why or why not?
7. What is your pastoral identity?
8. What do you do that makes you an organizational leader?
9. How do you self-differentiate in difficult situations involving congregants?

NOTES

1. William Willimon, *Pastor: The Theology and Practice of Ordained Ministry* (Nashville: Abingdon, 2002), 68.

2. Scott Thumma, Dave Travis, and Warren Bird, "Mega Churches Today 2005" (Hartford Institute for Religion Research and the Leadership Network, 2005), 1.

4. Ibid., 10.

5. Ibid.

6. Thomas Oden, *Pastoral Theology: Essentials for Ministry* (New York: HarperCollins, 1983), 52.

7. Gary L. McIntosh and Samuel D. Rima Sr., *Overcoming the Dark Side of Leadership* (Grand Rapids: BakerBooks, 2001), 22.

8. Murray Bowen, *Family Therapy in Clinical Practice* (Northvale, NJ: Jason Aronson, 1978), 355.

CHAPTER 2

Choosing the Work of the Associate Pastor

I remember one of my first hospital visits as an associate pastor. What was memorable was not the visit itself but the drive from the hospital back to the church. I was wearing a clerical collar because I was going into the intensive care unit of this hospital for the first time. I had wrestled with the decision to wear the collar. Some parishioners think it is too "Catholic." Other congregants like to see a minister in some type of distinguishing apparel. Often, however, I find it easier to wear a collar at a hospital. It wordlessly identifies me as clergy and allows me some professional courtesies. And that was an issue for me as a young associate pastor. Not only was I still struggling with finding my pastoral identity, but also I received some strange looks when I told people I was a pastor. "You are so young," they inevitably replied. "You don't look like a pastor." You can imagine the time I had to spend explaining myself. Sure, I love to interact with people, but being interrogated by Nurse Ratched is not the most pleasant experience!

As anticipated, the clerical collar alleviated my identity crisis at the hospital. It functioned as a uniform, allowing me to bypass the questions and doubts. But the solution to my identity crisis proved to be a double-edged sword.

After the visit, I got into my car and started to drive back to the church office. When I stopped at a traffic light before getting on the highway, I noticed a homeless man with a sign asking for money. He was walking up the line of cars and would soon approach my vehicle. Because I prefer not to hand out money without a complementary investment of time spent with the person in need, I resolved not to give the man any cash since I was not in a position to help him holistically. When the man passed my car, I did not roll my window down. Seeing my collar, however, the man became irate and started shouting at me.

I was relieved when the light finally changed, liberating me to drive away. The encounter left me shaken long afterward, however. Clearly, the man assumed that, as a pastor, I should have given him money. The same symbol of vocational identity that had facilitated my ministry at the hospital had become a stumbling block in my encounter with a homeless stranger.

When have you experienced a clash between identity (who you are as a pastor) and ministry (what you are called to do as pastor)?

Identity Crisis

Many associate pastors struggle with their identity in ministry. As associates, they are called to serve the congregation like any other pastor, but they do so in the role of number two (and sometimes number three or four) pastor. That functional hierarchy can generate an internal struggle as associates strive to discern and develop their position within the church or community. After all, aren't all pastors, whether associate or senior or solo, called to the same gospel work as servant leaders of God's people?

Calling

Just as a senior or solo pastor has a calling, so the associate pastor must have a calling. Calling is typically an individual's strong sense that he or she must move in the direction toward which God is guiding. Often college or seminary training is required along the way during the calling process. Many associate pastors are formally licensed and ultimately ordained, which is the biblical act of affirming that a person has been set apart by God for the ministry. Even in those churches that do not require an official process for licensing or ordaining associate ministers, it is highly recommended that leaders and congregations affirm the call of prospective associate pastors by examining their call to ministry, education, testimony, experience, spiritual life, and biblical knowledge.

A call to ministry can sometimes be construed to fulfill inadequacies in prospective associate pastors. In seminary, I witnessed many friends and acquaintances try to use ministry as therapy for their problems. Many who are unable to find instant acceptance at work, at home, or in their own community may seek to find gratification and respect through becoming a pastor. Churches are generally perceived to be places of love and acceptance, and too many congregations have been hurt by a pastoral leader working through their psychological baggage through their ministry. That is why the act of ordination requires congregations or denominational leaders to certify prospective pastors by interviewing, consulting, and discerning the call of individuals for ministry.

A Supportive Calling

Being called to a supporting or specialized role of pastoral leadership in the church is a demanding one. As suggested in the previous chapter, the associate pastor is called on to serve not only God's people but also the senior pastor, who is responsible for oversight of the larger ministry. Thus, the associate must be able to follow the direction and leadership of the senior pastor while maintaining leadership of his or her own ministry area.

Associate and senior pastors not only have the responsibility of leading the people of a congregation, but also are charged with the spiritual care of the church. Eugene Peterson calls this the care for the soul: "The soul is the essence of the human personality. The cure of souls, then, is the scripture-directed, prayer-shaped care that is devoted to persons singly or in groups, in settings sacred or profane."[1] Those in supportive ministry positions, including and especially associates, have to understand that they are physicians of the soul for the people in their congregations. Associates are often sought out by congregation members because they can be more accessible through their specialized congregational involvement. They are seen working within their ministry areas of children, youth, education, counseling, or music.

Associate pastors are not just servants; they are also leaders. It is natural for church staff and members to identify the senior pastor as the leader, but associates are also key leaders through their specialized ministries. Therefore, associates benefit from approaching their work in a spirit of humility and with an awareness of their own irrelevance. That was the lens through which Henri Nouwen understood pastoral work and Christian leadership. He stated that the example of Christ was that of humbleness and irrelevance.[2] It is the gospel message that is relevant. Pastors, senior or associate, are just the medium through which the gospel is proclaimed.

Christian leadership includes being centered in Christ daily. Associate pastors need to view their leadership through the lens of servanthood, which Christ displayed in the Gospels. Christ sought to guide people where they were in life, not where they should have been. This is the example of how associates must approach their specialized ministry when their job requires them to counsel and care for their congregation.

Callings of Associate Ministry

Associate pastors can have numerous specialties in many fields of work. The major categories of associate work are described below.

"Generic" Associate Pastor. These associates are often called assistant pastors because they perform many of the same duties of the senior pastor, including regular preaching, counseling, visitation, and teaching. These associates truly assist the senior pastor in the senior's day-to-day work. Often, these associates have supervision over two or three ministry areas, such as Christian education, missions, or youth work. Working as the "generic" associate pastor often produces a minister who ultimately becomes senior pastor of his or her own church.

Music Pastor. Depending on the church tradition, music pastors may be formally licensed or ordained to their specialized ministry. They frequently carry the title of "minister of music" or "director of music," and in addition to general ministry training, they are usually educated in instrumental and vocal music. Associates who work in music ministry provide vision, oversight, and musical direction in the life of the church for children, youth, and adults, including coordination with the preaching pastor for planning worship services. These associates usually direct and coordinate choirs, bands, worship teams, and instrumentalists. Music pastors are usually associates for the duration of their ministry, and in the majority of churches, they receive compensation for their work.

Youth Pastor. Associates in this specialized ministry are often recent college or seminary graduates with a passion for relating to youth—in part because they were youth themselves in the not so distant past! Those who desire to be youth pastors should be trained to understand the specialized nature of their work. They should understand how to make Scripture relevant to teenagers, and they should value communicating God's love for youth through fellowship and service projects as much as through teaching.

Beware of the candidate who assumes youth ministry is easy work or presumes to use it merely as a stepping stone to "more important" church ministry. In reality, youth ministry is one of the church's most important ministries because it focuses on the next generation of disciples. It is also demanding, challenging, and draining, and as a result, burnout is a common phenomenon for youth pastors. Although the average tenure of a youth pastor is just eighteen months, associates in this field of pastoral work can last for decades if proper support is given. However, it is common, especially among those with a seminary education, for these associates to move on to other pastoral work, including the senior or solo role.

Administrative Pastor. In many congregations, an associate pastor is specifically responsible for the managerial or organizational concerns of the church. In addition to seminary education, these associates may have training in the areas of management or human resources. Administrative associates are often individuals who performed this type of work in the secular sphere and now feel called to do the same work in the congregational setting. Administrative responsibilities typically include overseeing or coordinating with leadership boards such as the trustees or elders, working to improve staff relations, providing direction for lay leaders, and supervising day-to-day operations that occur on the church property.

Education Pastor. Education is often the cornerstone of a church through programs such as Sunday school, midweek Bible studies, and even church-sponsored day care, elementary or high schools, English as a second language (ESL) or tutoring services, and schools of ministry. Ideally, these associates should have training and experience in the field of teaching and education. These pastors oversee teaching staffs, both volunteer and paid, who equip the congregation with the learning needed to understand Scripture—and sometimes more. Usually the education pastor also teaches classes or groups that are offered year-round. If the church has a school, such as a preschool or elementary school, education pastors are often the administrators who provide the day-to-day supervision. Education pastors often stay in their field of specialized ministry for many years, and most are paid staff members. Some also become senior pastors who specialize in teaching and preaching.

Pastoral Care or Counseling Pastor. These associate pastors assist the senior pastor in leading a consistent and compassionate pastoral care ministry. This includes hospital visitation, pastoral counseling, support groups, individual counseling, care cards, bereavement care and funerals, and coordination of congregational care through deacons or trained lay shepherds. In a church with a counseling center, the pastoral care pastor may have administrative and clinical responsibilities related to the center. In many cases, it is expected that pastoral care pastors have specialized degrees in social work or counseling, and in most congregations, these specialized associates are salaried members of the pastoral staff.

Evangelism or Discipleship Pastor. Associates focused on evangelism and discipleship are concerned with growing churches numerically and spiritually. The main goal of such associates is to attract and maintain members and to deepen the faith of those who come to church. These supportive pastors often use special-interest programs or small groups to feed the spiritual needs of the congregation. These associates must be effective in interpersonal communication and usually need to train lay people to help lead the programs they create. Churches that include this type of associate among their leaders are usually prepared to pay a full-time salary for the role.

Children's Pastor. This specialized associate is charged with teaching and nurturing children to learn about God. Often, children's pastors are ministers with a degree in early childhood education and have training and experience that specifically address age-level learning. Associates who work with children also often oversee the church nursery or child care during church functions or worship. Meeting the needs of children's faith development is a special area of associate work for those who truly love children and want children to participate in the life of the congregation. Note that child protection policies are increasingly common in churches; many insurance companies and adjudicatory organizations require them. Therefore, children's pastors must not only have criminal and child abuse clearances themselves, but they must actively interview and screen volunteers. The children's pastor may need to educate other church leaders on mandatory reporting requirements of suspected abuse and the need for developing a protection policy.

Other Associates. Some associates operate beyond the traditional categories outlined above. They may have responsibilities in more than one of those areas (e.g., children and youth; education and evangelism/discipleship; worship arts [music, drama, dance, mime]), or they may be assigned more specialized ministries yet (e.g., singles ministry, seniors ministry, arts and recreation ministries). As congregations are unique and diverse from one another, so an equal or surpassing number of ministry portfolios may be assigned to associate pastors. All such ministry functions are intended to meet the needs of God's people and to further the reign of God in the world.

In some independent churches and in some traditions in the African American church among others, associates may have earned the title of "minister" based on their service as deacons or lay leaders or in recognition of less formal ministry training. These ministers generally have *not* been licensed or ordained through a formal process with a larger denominational or associational body. Often they have full-time or part-time jobs in non-ministry fields, and they serve in the role of associate minister without salary or other compensation from the church. These ministry leaders serve in a variety of roles, including one or more of the categories mentioned above. In the next chapter, there is further explanation about these associates. (That chapter also has a discussion about full-time and part-time and paid or unpaid associates.)

Vocational Tenure of Associates

The longevity of associates in a particular specialty area often varies because of the nearly universal tendency to "move up" in ministry as in every other field of work. Ministers move up to bigger churches or to higher positions in leadership. Nearly all pastors will experience some kind of transition or movement in their vocational journey. We move in response to God's call, in response to life transitions, and in response to family needs. Associate pastors are no different—and because of the more specialized nature of their work, they may move more often than the senior or solo pastor, sometimes in response to congregational needs and sometimes as a result of their own spiritual and personal development.

That being said, congregations may discover three primary types of associate pastors as it relates to their tenure of service.

The Professional Associate

First is the professional associate pastor. Professional associates stay within their specialized ministry for the duration of their career. For example, music and counseling pastors typically stay within their ministry field due to its focused nature. Furthermore, they may be required to earn a master's or even doctoral degree. Similarly, some youth pastors have been youth pastors for twenty-five years because they love what they do, and they know God desires that they stay in their ministry setting.

The professional associate can stay with a congregation for decades and may even outlast a senior pastor. These associate pastors enjoy their specialization of ministry and often exult that they do not have the senior pastor's worries about budgets, building projects, vision statements, managing staff, weekly preaching, and being the primary leader. Their dedication to their ministry specialty leads these associates to develop programs and accomplish goals related to their own area of expertise and passion.

Professional associates sometimes serve as models for their field. They may be asked to consult with other churches about building a particular area of ministry. One example of this is Darrell Pearson, a professor of youth ministry at Eastern University. He started out as a youth pastor and became so successful in that ministry that he was asked to teach at the college level. Today, Darrell also has his own consulting ministry to help churches grow or start a youth ministry.

Toe-dipping Associate

The second type of associate pastor in terms of longevity is typically a fresh-out-of-seminary graduate who wants to test the ministerial waters by dipping his or her toes in the associate pastorate pool. An associate position is an effective way for new graduates to learn, observe, and practice ministry in a supportive context, serving as a kind of apprentice to a more experienced senior pastor. Through the associate experience, these toe-dipping types are seeking to discern where God is calling them.

Often, learning from a seasoned senior pastor is the best way for associates to lead a church of their own in the future. These associates do not want to move up the ladder of pastoral work right away. They welcome the opportunity to learn in an environment where they are afforded room to grow, to try new ideas, and to fail. Having the ability to fail allows associates to learn firsthand what works and what does not work.

The associate who does not meet at least one failure in ministry has probably not been pushing the edge of what is possible in ministry. Before Thomas Edison perfected the light bulb, he learned from his mistakes and his failures to build one of the most important inventions of all time. It is beneficial for seminarians to practice the fundamental keys to successful ministry through an internship or field education before becoming a full-time associate pastor. However, new associates will need additional time and space to stretch their wings and take flight into the expanse of congregational ministries.

So, a note of exhortation to senior pastors: Resist the temptation to micromanage your associates during this early stage of exploration and innovation. The newly installed associate pastors will become frustrated by attempts to direct their day-to-day tasks, to govern the performance of duties previously mastered, or to insist upon your own way out of insecurity or a need for control. By taking the chance and trusting your new associate, you will create an environment where your associate will learn to trust not only you but also herself or himself. Know when to push and when to sit back so that the new associate can learn—but stay close enough to direct, encourage, or reassure when required.

Wait-and-See Associate

The third type of associate pastor might be called the wait-and-see associate. These associates feel called to ministry, but they may not know where their ultimate career goal will take them. Wait-and-see associates may sense a call to youth, education, or administrative ministry, but they often can't see themselves in that type of associate work for the rest of their career.

Some individuals who take the wait-and-see approach may be very good at a ministry specialty but want to discern whether their specialized ministry is truly what God desires for them. Other wait-and-see associates may sense a call to the solo or senior pastorate, but they know they are not ready to manage staff, provide the vision for a church, and be a confident leader.

Some wait-and-see associates remain in their associate role for several years, using the time to grow, discern, and prepare before looking to answer God's call to move on. Typically, associate pastors become effective in their assigned ministry after about three years of ministering in a single congregation. The most effective senior pastors are often associate pastors who have been successful in a specialized ministry before answering the call to become a head pastor.

Senior pastors and pastoral search committees should seek a clear picture from associate candidates about how long they desire to stay in associate ministry before moving on. Does the candidate anticipate a tenure of eighteen to thirty-six months? Or does she or he feel content in a specialized ministry setting and want to see that specialized call continue in the present congregation?

No matter the type of associate that enters a church, the church leaders responsible for overseeing the staff (most often a pastor/staff relations committee) should understand the associate's goals, dreams, and desires. Having open and honest communication about an associate's future is vital to the possible success of an associate's ministry. When church leaders understand where the associate wants to go in his or her ministry, the church can better prepare for transitions of associates, which leads to fewer disruptions to programs or ministries. Professional, toe-dipping, and wait-and-see associates are critical to the life cycle of each church that hires an associate minister. Ideally, churches should encourage associates to stay and provide consistency in programs and ministries, but sometimes associates leave because they sense that God is calling them elsewhere or they have answered the call to become a senior pastor. Consider carefully how God has called you to your place of ministry. Your circumstances may be challenging, but perhaps God is calling you to be a leader through a time of tension, congregational conflict, or healing.

Case Studies: Discerning God's Call

The following examples of individuals entering ministry are real situations experienced by ministry colleagues (whose names and personal details have been changed to protect their privacy). These examples represent the different courses that prospective associate pastors can take en route to the pastoral ministry. No one path to associate ministry is the right way, but each offers a different path on the journey to discerning God's call to ministry. The associate pastors introduced in these examples will serve as case studies in later chapters.

Case Study 1: Career Transition

Mike grew up in church and always enjoyed the music ministry. His teachers in school often encouraged Mike to seek a career in music, but Mike eventually went to a state college to study engineering. Throughout his undergraduate years, Mike enjoyed playing piano and singing in college and church choirs, but upon graduation he found a high-paying job in engineering. Several years went by. One day in church, Mike remembered how much he enjoyed church life, music, and serving others. Through several months of searching, discernment, and support from his wife, Mike enrolled in seminary to become a minister of music. Mike quit his engineering job and got a part-time job as a teacher of high-school music while his wife worked full-time. It took Mike five years to finish seminary, and when he did, Mike's home church ordained him. After being called to his first church, Mike felt relieved because he felt he had finally found his life's calling. It was a big step of faith for Mike, who would serve several churches as an associate minister of music and started music programs in each church.

Case Study 2: Response to an Early Call

Allison grew up in a large church with several associate pastors in various specialty areas. Allison felt God's call to ministry from an early age, but she did not know what kind of ministry God was calling her to. In her undergraduate years at a Christian college, Allison worked as a youth ministry intern at a nearby church. During her internship, Allison was able to serve in a number of other areas in the congregation, including visitation, teaching Sunday school, preaching, and supervising church volunteers. As graduation approached, Allison felt led to enter seminary to take the next step in discerning God's call for her ministry. Allison was able to relate her many experiences in church work to her seminary classes. In addition to her classroom education, Allison worked at a nearby church as assistant to the senior pastor of a large congregation. That pastor was a mentor to Allison and encouraged her to seek ordination, even serving as Allison's sponsor before the denominational board. When Allison graduated from seminary, she completed her examination with the denomination, was ordained, and accepted a position as an education associate. After thriving for ten years as an associate pastor, Allison felt God calling her to become a senior pastor in another congregation. Her internship, seminary education, and years as an associate had all prepared her for this ministry transition.

Case Study 3: From Retirement to Part-time Associate

Frank worked as a teacher for thirty-five years, faced retirement, and wondered how he would live out the rest of his life. At that time, Frank's church was identifying the need for another pastor to minister to a growing population of elderly members. The pastor of the church approached Frank about serving as a part-time associate pastor. At first, Frank was shocked. He had never been to seminary, so surely he could not be a pastor! Frank and his pastor met several times over a period of months to talk about the opportunity. The pastor noted Frank's effectiveness as a lay leader, particularly in the areas of visitation (on the church's care team) and education (as a Sunday school teacher). After much prayer and reflection, Frank agreed to serve his church as an associate pastor. He also decided to take some ministry classes at the local seminary but not to seek a master of divinity degree. The church and pastor agreed to hire Frank and ordain him after he completed the ministry classes. Frank spent many happy years as an associate pastor on a part-time basis and had a fruitful ministry.

Case Study 4: Lay Leadership as Training for the Pastorate
Kendra was active in her church and loved her church like a family. She was also chair of the deacon board. Her pastor had served for five years, and in that time the church grew to a point where another minister was necessary. However, because of budget shortfalls, the church was not able to hire another pastor. As the pastor analyzed his leaders, Kendra was a clear choice for becoming an associate pastor. Kendra's pastor approached her with the idea. She prayed and discussed the opportunity with her family. After many months of prayer and planning, Kendra became an unpaid associate working fifteen hours a week in the areas of visitation, discipleship, and education. After a period of a year, the congregation decided to ordain her to Christian ministry. As she worked toward ordination, Kendra attended ministry classes at the nearby seminary to equip her with the tools needed to be an associate pastor.

Discussion Questions for Churches
1. What is the important need in your church that is not being met? How might this need be fulfilled by an associate pastor?
2. What strengths do you look for in an associate pastor?
3. How might the calling of an associate pastor fit into your congregation's ministry goals and vision?
4. How much training or education do you expect a new associate pastor to have? In what area(s) would your associate(s) benefit from more training or education?
5. Which associate pastor type does your congregation have or

desire to have—professional, toe-dipping, or wait and see? In what ways can you encourage your associate(s) to make longevity a priority in your congregation?

6. What financial resources are available to pay an associate? Have you considered an unpaid associate pastor or commissioned lay leader to address ministry needs? Why or why not?

7. Research the opportunities provided to churches through grants or funded internships. What possibilities might become feasible with such resources?

Discussion Questions for Associate Pastors

1. What type of ministry do you feel God is calling you to in the future? What kind of ministry do you see yourself in one year? Five years? Ten years? Twenty years?

2. Do you sense that you need to stay in your current congregation? Why or why not?

3. Do you sense that you need to leave your current congregation? Why or why not?

4. How do you discern between God's call and your own selfish desires or ambitions?

5. What are the most important lessons learned as an associate pastor?

6. How have these lessons improved your effectiveness in the ministry?

7. What additional tools or support do you need to become the associate that God has called you to be?

NOTES

1. Eugene Peterson, *The Contemplative Pastor* (Grand Rapids: Eerdmans, 1989), 57.

2. Henri Nouwen, *In the Name of Jesus: Reflections on Christian Leadership* (London: Darton, Longman and Todd, 1989), 13.

PART TWO

Associate Ministry in Context

CHAPTER 3

Who Is an Associate Pastor?

Many congregations will have preconceived notions about the answer to this chapter's title question: Who is an associate pastor? Common assumptions are that the associate minister is young, probably fresh out of seminary, and eager to move up the leadership ladder, viewing the position of an associate as a first step toward the senior pastorate. For many churches, the assumption remains that the ministerial candidate will be male. One recent advertisement for an associate read, "A successful candidate for associate pastor is able to communicate God's word. *He* is able to connect with the flock" (emphasis added).

And yet, in the New Testament, Paul lists several women as his "fellow workers" or "colaborers," including Euodia and Syntyche. Phoebe and Priscilla were also notable leaders in the early church. Today in most mainline denominations, women are seen as equally called and qualified in the work of ordained ministry. However, even within those denominations, some congregations will balk at the idea of a female pastor. If a qualified female candidate should be presented to those congregations, the members or senior leaders may pass her over in favor of a male candidate. In other churches, the issue is less one of embracing a female associate and more one of affirming that woman's call to move into a senior pastorate—a phenomenon known as the stained-glass ceiling.

Similar discrimination may be found in the area of age and experience or ambition. Associates can be any age and often bring dynamic gifts and abilities to their specialized work. But even though the average age of seminary candidates is roughly 32 years old,[1] some churches may express surprise at an older candidate pursuing an associate position. Questions may arise about the aspiring associate's willingness to be supervised by a younger senior pastor or about why a veteran associate is content to remain in a subordinate role. So, perhaps the first answer to this chapter's question is, "The associate minister may not be the person you expect her (or him) to be."

The reality is that the demographic composition of associate pastors varies widely. For instance, according to the American Baptist Churches Information Service of the American Baptist Churches USA, the denomination's churches listed a total of 602 associates in 2012. Of those, 33 percent are female and 67 percent are male.[2] In 2010, the United Methodist Church had 4,156 clergy serving as associate pastors, or 14 percent of their total clergy.[3] Of those associates, 49 percent were women and 51 percent were men.[4] In 2011, the Presbyterian Church USA reported having 1,254 associates. Among those associates, approximately 49 percent are female and almost 51 percent are male.[5]

Church polity dramatically affects women serving in pastoral positions. For instance, the United Methodist Church explicitly allows for women to serve as pastor. In addition, United Methodist pastors are appointed by a bishop and churches do not have the ultimate authority to decide who their pastor should be. However, because of the polity of Baptist churches and others in the free-church traditions, each church has the authority to decide.

The Role of the Associate in the Congregation

When it comes to defining the role of an associate pastor, churches are often vague. General associates are typically given a few areas of responsibility but are sometimes seen as the person who picks up the missing pieces of their senior pastor. In contrast, specialized associate ministers, including those in the area of youth and music, usually have clear and somewhat obvious basic job descriptions, readily framed by their ministry title.

No matter what associate pastors are hired to do, however, they will ultimately find themselves doing too much if they do not have a clearly defined role. One associate pastor I spoke to lamented the fact that he does not have a job description; he was told only that he was the "education and youth guy." In addition, he has some general pastoral duties: leading worship, teaching Bible study, and occasional preaching.

Everyone in the church, from the senior pastor to the church member to the associate himself or herself, will benefit when the associate minister has a clearly developed job description, one that outlines what the associate should do and to whom the associate ministers. Without a job description, the associate must piece together her or his role in the life of the congregation, inevitably neglecting one area of ministry and stepping on toes in another. The senior pastor might work with the pastoral/staff relations committee and other church leaders to identify the greatest needs of the congregation and how the associate can minister in those areas. (Appendix A contains information about planning to hire an associate, and sample job descriptions can be found in Appendix B.)

Beyond a specific job description, the role of any associate pastor should encompass three key areas:

■ **Supporting the mission:** What is it that the congregation does in ministry? Does the congregation have a passion for mission, evangelism, music, outreach, community service, or youth? The successful associate is able to know the congregation's focus and how the members work within that focus.

■ **Supporting the vision:** What does the congregation want to become? The associate should be able to articulate the vision of the congregation and see himself or herself as an important player in that vision. The associate and the senior pastor need to work through a model that places the associate in the vision of what the congregation wants to become.

■ **Supporting the staff and church:** Is the associate a team player? As a pastoral staff member, the associate should work in cooperation with the senior pastor and/or other staff members but should not be micromanaged. Associates need to involve themselves with the ministries of their fellow staff members so that the congregation can be better served. The associate does not have to do someone else's job, but the associate should be engaged in all areas of church life. The associate should also support the church in causes. The music pastor should have a chance to go on a mission trip despite the fact that missions are not his or her ministry focus.

Keeping the associate involved in the larger church mission, vision, and staff decisions can aid an associate in feeling empowered and nurtured. When I interviewed several associates, each lamented about not being included into the greater life of the church. These associates observed that sometimes they feel relegated to their narrow areas of focus, such as family or education ministry. Ideally, associates will have a role in leading worship alongside the senior pastor every week and have regular opportunities to preach, to accompany the senior pastor to meetings, to lead in Communion, to participate in baptisms, to have a voice in congregational gatherings, and to initiate new ideas in their ministry areas.

The Role of the Associate in the Community

Associate pastors have opportunities in the community that their senior pastor may not have. Senior pastors are often focused on projects, church meetings, sermon preparation, worship planning, and other time-intensive endeavors and sometimes cannot connect to the community at large. Associates may have responsibilities related to outreach or evangelism and can position themselves to be actively involved in the community. When I was an associate pastor, I often attended community gatherings and local government meetings while my senior pastor was attending crucial congregational meetings. The senior pastor sent me to be the voice of the church because the congregation needed to be represented by a pastoral leader at such events.

Another way an associate pastor can be active in the community is through the local schools. One of the first things I did as a youth pastor was make an appointment with the principal of the local high school. As I met with the principal, I introduced myself as someone in the community who wanted to be involved with the school. Many of my youth were students at the school, and I wanted to be a presence in their extracurricular activities. I was aware, however, that schools increasingly discourage individuals other than parents from being on school property during school hours. Asking for the principal's permission to be around during and after school allowed me to be a welcomed presence rather than a suspicious stranger.

Months later, that meeting with the principal also positioned me to minister to the youth of my church and their friends in a special way. A tragic car accident occurred involving several students, and many were friends with the youth in my church. The school called me to serve as a grief counselor and allowed me to counsel dozens of students. I received calls and emails from parents thanking me for my ministry in the school that day. Much of the ministry I did that day, and in the days that followed, was being present in the school during a time of grief and loss. That would not have happened if I had never met with the high school principal.

Associates can be a presence in other areas of the community. Education pastors can connect with local teachers, libraries, and community centers to offer tutoring, mentoring, or workshops.

Music pastors can contact local bands or community orchestras to invite them to have concerts at the church or possibly involve church members in performances. Evangelism pastors can tap into local recreation leagues, business associations, public parks, civil organizations, YMCAs, or parenting groups to offer programs and activities that introduce the community to the local church. Associate pastors who have training in counseling can offer to serve as chaplains to police or fire departments, as well as at nursing homes and retirement communities.

When associates look to the broader community for avenues to minister through local groups, those pastors create opportunities of growth for the church. Looking beyond the four walls of the church can be a great way for churches to reach people in new ways. Associate pastors are uniquely positioned because of their gifts and flexibility of time.

The Role of the Nontraditional Associate

Religious leaders of the last few decades have pushed for the pastorate to be seen as a full-time profession, in addition to a vocational calling. However, full-time professional ministry may not be the calling for every associate or the need of all churches. Many congregations rely on unpaid volunteer ministers, part-time paid associate pastors, or bivocational pastors, and the issues of time and resources are often a challenge.

For associates falling into these categories, the term *nontraditional* may be used to distinguish part-time ministry from full-time professional associate ministry. Having to juggle two or more jobs can be difficult for associate pastors. Giving attention to the church's needs and being able to support yourself or a family can cause an associate to feel pulled in many directions. Some free churches, such as Baptist, Pentecostal, or Congregational churches, may not pay their associate clergy. This is especially common in many African American churches where precedent establishes that the title of "pastor" marks a distinction from that of associate minister, which may designate either licensed clergy or recognized lay leaders—or both. In mainline churches, these ministries may be handled by directors rather than pastors, and those directors may or may not be paid.

Much like their salaried counterparts, these unpaid associates often have specialized and respected roles, overseeing Bible studies, small groups, new member integration, visitation, Communion, and men's or women's ministries. These roles often develop because the congregation grows numerically or because the ministry vision expands in such a way that more leaders are needed to accomplish the church's goals.

When it comes to educational and ordination credentials for nontraditional associates, requirements vary across denomination, tradition, and culture. The free-church tradition lacks a hierarchical denominational system that typically dictates formal undergraduate or graduate-level education. That isn't to say that all or even most ministers and pastors in the free churches are uneducated! For example, there is freedom in the American Baptist Churches USA for a local church to ordain whosoever it deems to be called to gospel ministry, but the majority of congregations in the ABCUSA are part of regions or associations that have established educational and professional qualifications and a process for evaluating those qualifications before recommending a ministerial candidate for ordination by a local church. That process also secures the recognition of that ordination by the national body of ABCUSA.

Today, aspiring ministers can receive ministry training in a number of ways. Bible colleges, seminaries, ministry schools, and in-house church training are all sources of education for nontraditional associates. Although accredited college and seminary education is generally considered ideal, the cost and time of such an educational requirement is not practical for everyone. Depending on church polity, therefore, nontraditional associates may be licensed or ordained by the local church into pastoral or diaconate ministry.

Time and Compensation

As mentioned above, churches may have associates on a full- or part-time basis. Salaried professional associates are usually full-time ordained clergy at a church with a multi-pastor staff. The role of the full-time associate pastor takes more energy and more time than does that of a part-time associate, as the expectation is greater within churches that employ a full-time associate. Where the part-time associate has leadership over limited areas, the full-time associate usually has leadership over major responsibilities of the church. In large churches or megachurches, the music pastor is likely to have direction over all things music in the church. Education pastors will coordinate Sunday school, small groups, and education programs. The pastoral care pastor will have direction over the needs of church members and will provide care for those who are hospitalized, the infirm, and those requiring counseling. (Usually, these areas of church leadership require specialized education or experience.)

Sometimes, however, churches will choose to call one or more part-time associates, who may or may not be paid. Part-time associates in mainline churches are usually ordained clergy who are paid to serve in one or two areas of parish ministry for ten to twenty hours a week; generally these associates are also considered staff pastors. These positions may be filled by retired pastors or by clergy who are bivocational, often with a related career in teaching or counseling, or who have a spouse who works full time. Part-time associates in free churches may or may not be paid but typically serve in the same capacities as their mainline counterparts.

Part-time associates, whether they are paid or unpaid, must have a job description. Having specific boundaries of time and ministry area will reduce conflicts that revolve around the congregation's expectations of their associate minister. A job description will also focus the role of the part-time minister and will help the minister balance personal and ministry life in a healthy way (see Appendix B for a sample job description). In addition, paid part-time associates should have an agreement about office hours, Sunday commitments, evening commitments, and vacation. If the associate does not have an agreement, the time as a part-time minister can quickly add up to be a full-time job. (Chapter 8 discusses schedules for full-time and part-time associates.) Part-time associates, paid or unpaid, will find themselves attending some congregational meetings, leading in worship, and providing some pastoral care for the congregation.

Unpaid associates may struggle with separating the amount of time they work at church because volunteers in nonprofits lack clearly defined roles. In addition, part-time associates most likely serve in their own church and therefore are challenged by making a distinction between their work as a congregant and their ministry as an unpaid associate pastor. In free-church traditions, making the transition between congregant to unpaid associate is complicated because of the ambiguous expectations that churches have about volunteers.

Case Studies: Role and Responsibility

Case Study 1: Mike, a Minister of Music

Mike's role as the full-time, paid minister of music is to direct and grow the music ministry in his church. His duties include creating the bulletin for Sunday, preparing the choir for leading worship, coordinating the worship team, supporting leaders of the children's choirs, and designing new worship services. His direction from the senior pastor was clear: Mike was to take ownership of the music program. Beyond that, Mike was given freedom to begin new programs and musical groups that added to the already dynamic music program at his church. Mike's role was critical in the church. As the chief musician, his leadership would guide those in the music ministry into a place where more people could be involved and seek a greater connection to Christ through music. Mike took this role as a minister of music seriously. His commitments to music, to Christ, and to the church were important. Mike's senior pastor gave him latitude to be able to take the music program in a direction that would include the congregation into more profound music and worship.

Case Study 2: Allison, a General Associate

Allison was hired to serve as a full-time general associate at First Church. Her role was to support the senior pastor in the areas of preaching, teaching, pastoral care, and administration of the church. Often, the senior pastor would travel to conferences, speak at denominational events, and give ministry training seminars. The church needed another staff pastor to fill his role at these times. Allison had had a strong internship that prepared her for such a role. She would preach about once a month, visit church members, and attend congregational meetings when the senior pastor was away. She had to know and understand the ongoing programs, concerns, and ministries of the church and be able to direct and guide when the senior pastor was away on vacation or attending a conference.

Case Study 3: Frank, an Educational Specialist

Frank, as a retired teacher, had a lot of experience in education. This provided a solid background for his role as a part-time paid educational associate pastor in his home church. Though he did not have a graduate-level degree, his ministry classes at a local seminary provided the ministry know-how necessary for an associate pastor. Frank's senior pastor asked him to develop a new small-group ministry. Frank was able to use his experience as an educator to recruit, train, and support the small-group leaders.

The senior pastor directed Frank to provide small groups for youth, adults, and senior adults. The senior pastor worked closely with Frank to marry Frank's expertise in education and his inexperience in pastoral ministry. Through there were some struggles, Frank was able to establish a well-received small-group ministry in the church. The senior pastor was involved in every step in Frank's development, which led to a fruitful ministry for the church.

Case Study 4: Kendra, Coordinating Paid and Unpaid Work
Kendra, as an unpaid associate, was directed by her senior pastor to guide the areas of Sunday school and visitation in their church. Kendra also had a part-time job as a community center coordinator. She often would split days as a coordinator of the local activity center and as an associate pastor. In addition, Kendra is a mother of two teenage children. Her ministry of visitation to church members in the hospital and to shut-ins was a welcomed addition to the church. The senior pastor in the church was also a local Bible college professor and was not able to make as many visitations as the church would like. Kendra was able to meet the pastoral needs of the congregation and promote the church's Sunday school and educational programs. Kendra's role as an unpaid associate was an effective model for the church because it allowed the church to provide care in the areas where the senior pastor could not without adding a financial burden to the small congregation.

Discussion Questions for Churches
1. What role(s) does your associate pastor fill in your church? Or, what role(s) could an associate pastor fill in your church?
2. How can the church's leaders better clarify the role(s) of an associate in the church?
3. In what ways does (or could) an associate fulfill the mission of the church? How does (or could) an associate support the vision of the church?

4. In what role(s) might the church benefit from a part-time associate? from a full-time associate?

5. How does (or could) your associate participate in the community? How might such participation meet the needs of the community? How might it benefit the church?

6. In what additional areas could an associate serve?

7. How does your associate(s) work with the other leaders of the church?

8. How does the associate's role in the church improve the church's passion for ministry?

9. In what ways are you currently developing associates in your church? What can you do differently to better support your church's associate(s)?

10. Ask congregants to describe the work of your associate(s). What words do they use to describe their ministries?

Discussion Questions for Associates

1. What is your role in your church? How clearly is it defined?

2. Name three ways that you support the vision of the church in which you serve. Does it match what the senior pastor desires? Why or why not?

3. To what extent and in what ways are you involved in the community?

4. What is your biggest challenge as an associate in the church?

5. What factors negatively affects your role in the church?

6. What factors positively affects your role in the church?

7. How has your role changed over time in your ministry?

8. What resources are available to you to make your ministry more effective?

9. How often do you and the senior pastor meet to discuss the church's vision? Do you discuss how you fit into that vision? Why or why not?

NOTES

1. "More young adults going into ministry," *USA Today*, September 9, 2010.

2. American Baptist Churches Information Service, June 2012.

3. General Commission on the Status and Role of Women in The United Methodist Church, "Clergywomen in Local Churches", *The Flyer* 37, no. 2 (April–June 2006), 8.

4. Ibid., 9.

5. Presbyterian Church USA, "Associate Pastors in the Presbyterian Church (U.S.A.)," Research Services, February 2012. www .pcusa.org/media/uploads/research/pdfs/associate_pastors_ report_and_appendix.pdf (accessed June 11, 2012).

CHAPTER 4

How Do Associate Pastors Minister?

Many associates struggle to find their identity in a ministry of a church. Those searches for identity can be confusing and frustrating. Depending on the focus or job description of an associate pastor, the ways in which that associate functions will tend to vary. Generally, an associate supports a few specific areas of church ministry. As considered in previous chapters, those areas may be closely related to each other, such as evangelism and outreach or discipleship and education. Other areas may be specific to the associate's training and expertise, such as music, children and youth, or pastoral counseling. Other associates may be assigned areas based on the felt needs of the senior pastor or the congregation, whether serving as a generalist or tasked with community outreach or pastoral care because of the senior pastor's other areas of focus.

Note, however, that after identifying a ministry niche, associates are wise to remain flexible in their function. Even an administrative or executive associate will need to learn best pastoral care practices because no associate pastor will stay locked in an office and never see a single soul. All associates need to be able not only to excel in their focus area but also to gain a breadth of pastoral skills that will maximize their touch on people's lives.

Functioning in Light of Ministry Focus

To highlight the ways in which associate pastors minister, I conducted several interviews with associates. Emily Earnshaw is associate pastor at Cañon City First United Methodist Church in Cañon City, Colorado. Emily outlines how she ministers:

> Adult Christian education is my primary area. However, this includes a large range of tasks including preaching once a month, visitation, teaching Bible study every other week, and leading the Christian education team toward fulfilling their vision of meeting people where they are and helping them know Christ. Their chosen mission is, "Through every offering of Christian Education when people come with the world in their head, they will leave with Jesus in their heart." We coordinate traditional Sunday school experiences, small groups, and upcoming events called our "Speaker Series."

Although Emily's ministry focus is adult Christian education, general pastoral duties are part of her work because her church seeks to include her in full pastoral leadership. She shares some leadership with the laity and is responsible for accomplishing vision goals.

Some associates are used in more general ways. Jennie Barrett Siegal is associate pastor at a traditional mainline congregation with active ministries of children, youth, and adults. Jennie describes her full-time paid ministry position:

> I'm lucky enough to have a generalist position, so I'm involved with worship leadership and preaching, adult education, pastoral care, reaching out to visitors and new members, and stewardship. The only part of our church's ministry that I'm not involved with is the youth group. I really enjoy being part of a ministry team. I am most excited by the opportunity to lead and vision and brainstorm along with colleagues. I find it particularly

challenging to envision and imagine the church's future in isolation—it's much more fun to do that with a team.

Leading as a team is a fruitful ministry practice. When associates are seen as colleagues rather than underlings, churches benefit from the unity of the staff. Jennie's function in the church takes many forms, and she serves as the senior pastor's right hand. An environment in which staff members work together can lead to a dynamic of iron sharpening iron, in which all parties benefit from sharing ideas.

Other associates may serve in an executive or administrative role. An executive associate oversees the administration of the church and many of its day-to-day operations. This often allows the senior pastor to focus on preaching, teaching, public speaking, denominational service, and vision for the church. Don Hanshew, formerly an executive associate pastor at Fountain City United Methodist Church in Knoxville, Tennessee, explains his role:

> I had responsibility for all program ministry and staff, local ministry outreach, support for all three worship services, and served on all administrative and executive boards. It was exhausting and at the same time invigorating to see how the sum of a properly aligned team could be much larger than the parts.

Duties in Worship

Depending on the size of a congregation, associates many have a great deal of responsibility in worship. In smaller churches, the associate pastor may lead aspects of worship that do not require much preparation time, including the call to worship, greetings, children's message, serving Communion, or taking the offering. Their role in worship may vary from leading music to guiding the congregation through a prayer time. Regardless of what the associate does in worship, it is important that the congregation understands the associate as a co-laborer in the ministry of the church. Visual placement of the associate during worship is one of the ways senior pastors can communicate this equality. Thus, associates often sit in the pulpit or chancel area, or in churches with a large number of associates the senior pastor might encourage them to sit in another area designated for leaders, including the deacons or elders.

As far as preaching goes, churches vary widely in the role they allow their associates. Senior pastors may perceive associates to be young upstarts, and some associates may indeed be ambitious. These perceptions and feelings may lead to anxiety for seniors and associates alike when it comes to sharing a pulpit, which is often a symbol of pastoral authority in the church. However, one way to alleviate anxiety and avoid a power struggle is for churches to put in place job descriptions for their associates. The job description becomes a basis for congregants and staff to understand clearly defined ministry roles.

Sharing the preaching responsibilities accomplishes two things for the congregation. First, it enables the primary preacher to rest. Even if the senior pastor preaches lights-out sermons and dozens of people come to Christ every week, the senior pastor also needs rest. If associates are assigned preaching duties 4 to 6 times out of 52 weeks per year, the associate is preaching 7 to 11 percent of the time. Weeks when the associate pastor preaches are weeks when the senior pastor can focus on tasks that are often neglected when a sermon deadline looms: visiting shut-ins, planning for vision statements or preaching, professional development, and ministry training for lay people.

Second, when the senior pastor shares preaching duties, the congregation perceives that leadership responsibilities are balanced. When congregants see the senior pastor listening to a sermon given by an associate pastor, this communicates to them that the senior pastor is someone who does not need always to be in control. Also, it displays the talents of the associate and thus reflects the positive effect that the senior has on the church as a whole by keeping and leading such a talented associate. Obviously, associates can also preach when the senior pastor is away, but the presence of the senior pastor allows him or her to give helpful feedback and coaching.

If the associate is not particularly strong in the area of preaching, then the church can arrange for the associate to attend conferences, classes, and seminars on preaching and homiletics. Nevertheless, the associate needs to be given opportunities to share and preach the Word of God in public.

In addition to preaching, opportunities for associates to serve the ordinances or sacraments are also important. The sight of multiple clergy serving or presiding over the Communion elements helps the congregation understand the priestly function of a pastor, an inherent ministering aspect of every clergyperson.[1] This visual also encourages the congregation to see the associate as a trusted pastor who serves alongside the senior pastor in shepherding the church. It shows the congregation that the associate and senior can work together as they share the gifts that God gives to us through the experience of Communion.

Baptism is another event that associates are able to perform. Often, associates will perform baptisms of persons in the congregation because they have played a part in that person's faith development. Additionally, the associate can perform baptisms with the senior pastor. If there is a liturgy for baptism, then the liturgy can be shared among the clergy.

Weddings are also a part of the church's worship. The senior pastor may be the main officiant at weddings, but participation in wedding services by associates is another picture of clerical unity within the life of the church. One of the most meaningful aspects of an associate pastor's development is involvement in congregants' life events. Relegating associates to minor religious duties tends to delay their growth as ministers of the gospel and minimizes their value and perceived competency in the eyes of the congregation. This is especially true for younger clergy who often take years to embrace their identity as a religious leaders and who may need to work hard to gain the respect and trust of church members.

Working Together

If a church has a particularly large staff of associates, the associates have opportunities to work with one another in exciting and creative ways. The youth pastor and the music pastor can plan outreach events and retreats that draw youth or young adults to be active in the church. The education and discipleship pastors can work together on programs, classes, and activities that feed the spiritual and educational growth of congregants. As a young person, I attended retreats in my church that were jointly planned and run by two associate pastors. Seeing them work together and have fun together taught me what quality adult friendships and working partnerships are like. These two associates not only modeled how to build healthy friendships in general but also taught me how to form constructive and collaborative relationships with other associates. An even more powerful illustration of a healthy staff model was when the senior pastor attended and participated in the retreats. The senior pastor allowed the associates visible autonomy with the way the retreat was planned and run, thus freeing the senior pastor to interact with the students in a relaxed way that formed powerful bonds of trust.

On a multi-pastor staff, ministering in mutuality can help the church grow. Some church staff environments can create competition among associates. If associates are consistently driven by senior pastors who want to see results only in numbers, then pastors can expect to see burned-out associates. If pastors can work together to accomplish goals, then associates will tend to have longer pastorates and more successful ministries.

Function as a Family

In the last several years, seminaries and ministry schools have focused on family systems theory. Murray Bowen proposed that individuals cannot be understood only individually, but rather as a part of their family as an emotional unit.[2] There are similarities between how families function and how churches operate, and this systems approach provides insight when it is applied to churches. Families and organizations are systems of interconnected and interdependent individuals, systems which cannot be understood in isolation. Associates entering a church should understand that when they become a pastor, they are entering a complex system of relationships, actual families, conflict, narrative, emotional triangles, assumptions, and expectations.

In order to minister effectively, associates will find family systems thinking helpful in equipping themselves to relate in healthy ways to their ministry peers and to church members. Three major arenas of family systems can aid all of us in team ministry: triangles, non-anxious presence, and boundaries.

Triangles

Triangles can occur between church members, between staff members, and among church members and staff. Person 1 has a history of conflict with Person 2 over the placement of the Bible in the sanctuary. Person 1 seeks out an authority figure, the worship pastor, to further establish her or his position. The attention is now focused on the worship pastor teaming up with Person 1 against Person 2. Often pastors do not realize that they have been caught in triangulation until they are deep into conflict. This dynamic is particularly destructive when a congregant or staff member involves two pastors in the triangle—and it may be yet more destructive when one is the senior pastor and the other an associate. Avoiding these triangles in healthy ways enables people to solve problems on their own. Associate pastors can be a source of advice in a conflict involving two parties without taking sides—whether against a ministerial colleague or against another congregant. Associates can see such triangles forming when these kinds of questions are asked by others:

> "Don't you think I'm right?"
> "Stephen is always putting me down. Can you do something about it?"
> "Can you help me fight this battle?"

Or, questions may not be asked, but subtle comments may rope associates into a triangle:

> "I'm not good with conflict. I guess I'll just let this go unless someone steps in."
> "Who can help? Well, I'll just keep losing in this argument as I always do."
> "No one ever sticks up for me."

The associate may feel guilt, remorse, pity, or a need to take sides. However, healthy ways of dealing with conflict enable all parties to put in equal work and resolve issues.

An Example of Triagulation

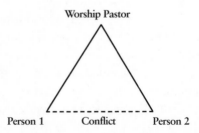

Worship Pastor

Person 1 · · · Conflict · · · Person 2

Non-Anxious Presence

Using the family systems approach, associates need to recognize an anxious presence: that person who operates from a position of nervous reaction to change or challenge. An anxious presence could be a lay leader who cries "fire!" at every difficulty or juncture. This dynamic can create a heightened over-awareness for pastors who believe that they must reactive immediately to every problem. This creates added and unwanted stress on the associate.

Associate pastors may receive a great deal of direction from senior pastors—or almost none at all. Both dynamics can be stressful for the associate, who may begin to doubt, question, and emotionally react to the senior pastor's emotions. The relationship of the senior and associate becomes a complex emotional mixture of sharing authority in the church. In congregational systems, a challenge to who has and controls the authority is a recipe for disaster. Unhealthy dynamics of power, rivalry, and control often create a system of organizational anxiety. Anxiety may become internalized and steer the associate into greater stress. The internal feelings come to a head, and the internal becomes external. The associate begins sharing these feelings with parishioners. Now the parishioners are anxious because they believe there is friction between the senior and associate pastors.

Managing such anxiety and stress is critical for associate pastors. Associates can manage stress in a variety of ways: exercise, journaling, talking to a confidential third party who is not related to the associate's church, or engaging in a hobby. Participating in clergy groups and respite ministries can aid the associate in processing the stress of anxiety. Being a non-anxious presence in ministry requires an individual to care for their congregation enough to not bring their stress into their role as an associate.

Boundaries

Healthy boundaries in ministry are a complex matter. Often pastors, especially associates who are new to the community or congregation, allow themselves to open their entire life to the church. All of their close friends are found in the church, but how can pastors in crisis get the help and accountability they need if their entire support network consists of church members? When the crisis concerns another church member or the church at large, to whom can the pastor turn? Pastors need to be able to separate their intimate relationships from the church.

Another boundary issue is related to "playing favorites." An associate may feel particularly connected with a small group of parishioners, but caution is advised about how much time is spent with a single group of church members. Boundaries are especially important when sexual attraction exists. Constant evaluation on the part of the associate is in order, and ministerial colleagues may also offer insight and accountability. Boundaries of closeness to individuals should look something like this:

Levels of Intimacy in Relationships

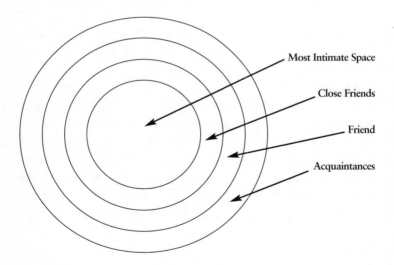

Most Intimate Space

Close Friends

Friend

Acquaintances

As depicted in the graphic, the smaller the circle, the fewer the number of relationships within it and the more intimate those relationships. As you progress to the outer circles, your relationships become less intimate and greater in number. Usually in our relationships, we disclose the intimate details of our life to a small group of people: immediate family, a spouse, or a few close friends might know almost everything about us. Usually we spend the most time with these trusted people.

In terms of our church ministry, the better our boundaries, the more effective our ministry. Thus for pastors, including associates, it is healthy and prudent to cultivate friendships outside of the church as well as within it. Members of our extended families, friends from childhood or school, or ministerial colleagues from our tradition or other traditions may be among those we turn to for companionship, understanding, or wise counsel. Establishing a middle ground with our time is key to establishing healthy boundaries—not only by setting limits on congregational intimacy but by carving out time for our own families.

Family Systems at Work in the Church

Using a family model is helpful to understand staff dynamics in church, not because the comparison of the church and family systems theory is ideal but because many churches have dysfunctions that are comparable to familiar family dysfunctions. And just as understanding your family of origins can empower you to make healthier choices for yourself and your family, so understanding the system of relationships within your church can equip and empower you as an associate to be a better servant leader.[3]

Paul's teaching of the essential "members of the body" passage in 1 Corinthians 12 helps us understand how the individual member of a family or system is critically important. This concept of being members to a body has clear connections how members of families, teams, and churches function. The comparison that Paul illustrates using the parts of the body (hand, eye, and ear) provides us with a theology of how one individual, in a system of individuals, can have positive and negative effects on the system. For Paul, the eye cannot cause amputation of the hand because the effects would be devastating to the body. Indeed, as Paul writes in verse 14, "Now the body is not a single part, but many." Using this connected systems approach to the church body clues pastors into how boundaries of individuals within the system help produce a healthier "body" of believers.

The authority structure that is often unbalanced or abused in a family has interesting parallels with the authority structure that is shared in a church. Scripture teaches that the "head" of the church is Jesus, but in many congregations today, the senior pastor may assume that role in unhealthy ways. In families children are to obey their father or mother. Parents are the ones who enforce rules, traditions, and patterns for living and guide the children in discipline. For churches, the senior pastor may be the leader in many of these areas, but it would be hard to support biblically the role of pastor as parent and parishioners as children.

Primarily family-systems thinking helps a ministry team see a bigger picture with a clearer view of the organization's dysfunctions. Often, when conflict with one team member exists, we tend to believe it is that team member who is the problem. However, in reality, a mosaic of influencing factors exists, just as in a family therapy scenario.

For instance, a person seeks counseling for her or his failure to form healthy relationships. Instead of seeing that person as the center and sole source of the problem, a therapist trained in family systems theory would ask the client about parents, siblings, and other family members. If a pattern emerges that indicates relationships within the family function in unhealthy ways, the therapist may begin to understand the client's issues as a lifelong problem. Deeper issues are involved than just bad choices in adult relationships; these issues may arise from a consistent learned behavior from the client's family of origin. Since the first third of our lives are the most formative years of learning and growing, the behaviors, patterns, and ways of interaction with others are often repeated throughout our lives.

Applying this framework, we understand how a church staff interacts, especially when it comes to the ministry of associate pastors. If a church's model of team ministry includes viewing the senior pastor as the source of authority and the associate pastor as subordinate, we can begin to uncover why unresolved conflict occurs. The goal of this book is to break any rigid ministry model in which the senior pastor becomes the dictator and the associate is the underling. A healthy model of associate ministry sees the associate as a fellow laborer in the work of the church. True, there must be some supervisory components in the relationship, but the relationship of the senior and the associate is most effective when stemmed from a position of mutuality and not animosity.

In family systems thinking, there is an interrelationship of how conflict begins, sustains, and comes to a conclusion. As with organic families, conflict is met and handled within a system. Churches and pastors are no different. Ronald Richardson, in *Creating a Healthier Church*, lists four patterns of reactivity to conflict: compliance, rebellion, power struggle, and emotional distancing.[4] I have summarized his discussion of these patterns below.

Compliance / This acceptance is generally forced to maintain the status quo. Ending conflict in this way breeds resentment and anger. Associates experience this when a senior forces compliance rather than fosters mutual acceptance. Going along with the state of affairs usually helps minimize conflict on staffs but leads to bitterness and resentment.

Rebellion / This is the opposite of compliance and exists when the associate says or does the antithesis of what the senior pastor or congregation requests. Acting out this way creates tension that is public and usually messy. Having a purpose, a plan, and a vision for the associate's work can make her or his job more purposeful.

Rebellion may also occur when too much compliance builds up. The compliant associate may emotionally channel the negative energy of accrued resentment and anger into a rebellious act. Associates may also have an inclination to rebel when they believe that they have the right ideas or the right plans.

Power Struggle / Rebellion may be a current running through this particular pattern, but power struggles are usually more ongoing and more destructive. While rebellion may be a one-time act, usually a public and aggressive one, a power struggle may be waged under the radar and over a long period of time. Passive aggression is often the modus operandi, which is more difficult to pinpoint and confront. In a power struggle, both the senior and the associate label each other as wrong, cut each other off emotionally, and act on their frustrations, all of which breed antagonistic actions. Clearly, motives of a power struggle may begin with "what's best for the church" but ultimately go far beyond to become more of an individual's crusade for power, acceptance, or control. Power struggles may arise from feelings of jealousy or fear, or from a lack of self-esteem. These insecurities foster an attitude of inadequacy when one pastor compares himself or herself with another. A senior pastor may lament his style of preaching because the youth pastor is more dramatic in her presentation; such a charismatic presence may be perceived as a direct attempt to seize control of the congregation. Lay leadership may attempt to gain control of a church and directly challenge a pastor and a pastor's ability to lead. In any power struggle, triangulation occurs in an attempt to build a coalition of supporters so that it is a force of many instead of one or two critics.

Emotional Distancing / This is often the last option for associates. This behavior is employed by associates who don't know how to handle the conflict. Emotional distancing can take any form but could present itself when an associate decides not to show up for church meetings or for a meeting with the senior pastor. Avoidance is the name of this game. Associates who emotionally distance themselves no longer desire to deal with conflict because it is exhausting or because they see it as a lost cause.

Richardson takes these approaches and applies them to how church members deal with conflict. I believe the responses are identical to how associates and senior pastors deal with their differences. Associates would be well advised not to take a position of seeing the conflict as the other person's problem. Instead, the question for associates to ask is, "By my action or inaction, how am I contributing to this problem?" That question requires considerable maturity to answer and should be explored with an outside trusted colleague.

Case Studies: Associates Ministering in Light of Their Focus

Case Study 1: Building Trust with Youth in Music Ministry

Mike works as the music pastor at a medium-sized church. His weekly duties include directing the choir and praise team and leading in worship on Sunday mornings. He ministers to musicians and volunteers within the music ministry. Mike is actively involved in the lives of the youth in the church who are also part of the youth praise team.

Mike's church has a youth minister on staff. After talking with the youth minister about a troubled teenager, Mike decided to seek out the youth to ask him how he was doing. At first, the youth did not want to share his personal issues with Mike. Mike, as the music pastor, wanted to find a way to connect with this troubled youth. After some initial conversations,

Mike discovered that the youth was interested in music, particularly guitar. A new worship service was beginning on Sunday nights, and Mike needed a guitar player to fill out the praise team. The youth was invited to play guitar for the service. Mike began to build trust and rapport with the youth, and the teenager opened up about his personal struggles. Mike knew that his role as the music pastor made him someone who could connect with this young person. Rather than push the issue and try to dig, Mike built trust and encouraged the youth to open up. Mike's ministry with music has a general benefit to the church, but Mike is able to use his specific skills to counsel and affirm the youth.

Case Study 2: Ministry That Followed from Social Work

Kendra, an unpaid associate pastor at her church, works thirty hours a week at the community center as a social worker. Many families from the community also come to her church's food pantry. Though Kendra does not serve in the food pantry on a weekly basis, she is responsible for running that ministry. She trains volunteers, schedules pantry workers, applies for grants to fund the pantry, and sometimes meets with families for special food needs.

As a social worker with the city, Kendra comes into contact with many of the families that come to her church for assistance. Kendra began to help a family find housing through her social work but quickly realized that the family needed more. Using her skills as a social worker, Kendra established a ministry at her church that taught low-income workers basic computer and office skills to encourage them to find higher-paying jobs. Because Kendra had contacts through her social work, she was able to create a successful ministry meeting the needs of hundreds of families in her community. Using the skills in her day job shaped her ministry to families who came to the food pantry. Parlaying her contacts, resources, and knowledge of how to contact people in help agencies turned into a thriving ministry for her congregation.

Case Study 3: Expertise and Calling as an Asset to the Church

Frank, a former schoolteacher, became a part-time associate pastor of education with senior adults in his home church. During his teaching career, Frank had been chair of the social studies department at the local high school. Frank had experience supervising staff and other teachers in the social studies department. The church needed to strengthen its Christian education program. After talking with the senior pastor about the vision of Christian education in the church, Frank decided to offer Sunday school and weekly educational opportunities. Frank began to recruit and train teachers for child, youth, and adult educational classes and groups. After preparing the church for a new educational program for more than six months, the new classes were welcomed with much anticipation and support. Frank's experience with education was well-paired with his calling as an associate pastor. His skills and gifts blended into an asset for the church. Ministering in light of his focus was supported by the church and the senior pastor because Frank's gifts and the church's needs matched well.

Discussion Questions for Churches

1. In what ways does your associate(s) participate in the larger functions of the church?

2. Ask if your associates would like to function in ways that may be outside their current job description. Discuss their ideas and create an action plan for enlarging or adapting their role(s).

3. In what ways does your senior pastor make the associate(s) a "coworker in the ministry"?

4. How does each associate pastor participate in worship (if at all)? In what other areas might the associate(s) be utilized?

5. How does the work of the associate(s) in worship allow the

congregation to see the associate participating in the life of the church?

6. How often does the congregation hear the associate preach? Is it enough? Why or why not?

7. Using family systems theory, describe how your congregants relate to one another and to your associates.

8. How well does the associate function with other church staff members? What is done well? What needs improvement?

9. How does your associate handle differences of opinion, style, theology, or communication?

10. When tense issues arise in the life of the church, how does your associate help or hinder the process of resolving conflict?

Discussion Questions for Associates

1. How do you feel about your ministry and ministry focus? Does the church know what you do? Why or why not?

2. What would you consider to be the recipe for success in your ministry?

3. How are your gifts affirmed or not affirmed in the church?

4. What other ministry areas are related to your focus as an associate?

5. How do you get caught in triangles? How do you get out of triangles?

6. How do you respond to conflict with individual congregants? with staff? Why do you respond this way?

7. How does family systems thinking challenge the way you minister?

8. How do you handle anxiety? How does it spill out into the congregation?

9. How does viewing your church and its ministry team as a family change the way you understand your congregation?

10. What is the greatest strength of your ministry? What is your greatest weakness?

NOTES

1. Please read William Willimon's *Pastor: The Theology and Practice of Ordained Ministry* (Nashville: Abingdon, 2002) for more on this concept of "pastor as priest."

2. Murray Bowen, *Family Therapy in Clinical Practice* (Northvale, NJ: Jason Aronson, 1978).

3. Ibid.

4. Ronald Richardson, *Creating a Healthier Church* (Minneapolis: Fortress, 1996), 93-95.

CHAPTER 5

Where Can You Find Associates?

When I was an associate pastor, I heard of another church nearby that was struggling to remain relevant in a changing community. What had started as a small rural community had begun to change into an outer ring suburb. There was a small church on a corner of two roads in the town. The congregation was small, but it was led by a faithful group of long-time church members. As shops, stores, and housing built up around the church, the congregation had a choice: Do we grow with the area, or do we remain who we are? The congregation struggled with questions of vision and mission in light of the changing community. A family who founded the church wanted the congregation to remain small and rural even though there was change all around the church. Many in the congregation left because they felt that the church should take the next step and begin to refocus its ministry.

For many churches, the primary goal is keeping the church open. Many congregations cannot even think about a vision because they are so focused on paying bills for the next six months. However, churches that choose to take a risk and embrace the possibility of change often make a first step in that direction by welcoming a new pastoral staff member, typically an associate pastor.

Especially for a congregation that is faltering in the face of economic hardship and community shifts, it requires much faith and planning to add a pastoral staff member. Budget impact is the number one concern: "How can we afford another pastor?" Many churches think they are not big enough. This is where the role of the nontraditional or the unpaid associate often comes into play. The good news is that a variety of ministry organizations (e.g., Fund for Theological Education, the Lilly Foundation, Christian schools of ministry on seminary campus, and emerging accredited online ministry programs), can guide churches through this process and even help them find funding through outside sources. The size of the church does affect an associate's role and work, but different-sized churches can sustain an associate pastor to feed the flock or support a vision for growth.

Types of Churches

Every year we hear all sorts of statistics about church size. We read about churches growing, churches dying, or churches stabilizing. We hear that half the churches in this country average fewer than one hundred people in attendance. As a result, we may assume that half the churches in this country are small and the other half are large. However, there is a wide spectrum of church sizes, and each congregation will face distinct challenges directly related to size.

A smaller church, for instance, may feel more connected because everyone knows one another in the congregation. People in a large congregation may not feel as connected to their fellow members, but the church is able to minister to hundreds, perhaps thousands of people. The goal here is not to argue which church is more effective at reaching people. Rather, the goal is to survey church sizes to examine how associate pastors can be effective in a variety of environments. The following is a breakdown of church sizes and how an associate pastor can be utilized in each one.

House Church

The concept of the house church goes back to New Testament times. Early Christians met in someone's home for worship and encouragement. Often, the threat of persecution caused these Christians to meet privately or even secretly in a member's home, but in some instances, house churches formed because the number of Christians in a town was easily accommodated in a private home.

In contemporary society, many churches start in someone's home. Churches of this size do not normally have an associate pastor because these congregations range from four to twenty people. House churches may not have an ordained or salaried pastor. They may be led by someone with Bible-school education or ministry training. Being able to pay one pastoral leader in a house church may be a challenge in itself. And in practical terms, only the largest house churches would have need for an associate in light of the low pastor-to-member ratio! So, while not impossible, it is unlikely that an associate would be called to a house church.

Family Church

These congregations have anywhere from twenty to seventy active members. Family churches are so named because the modest membership is closely connected. Often, the church is made up of several families who are related, if not by birth and marriage then by shared experience. These prominent families run the day-to-day operation of the church, leaving the pastor to function in more limited ways (as preacher and officiant at key events such as weddings, funerals, baptisms, and Communion). These churches are notable for having a matriarch and patriarch with well-respected and established roles, and because of the tight familial ties among the members, change is slow to take effect in these churches.

Clergy who pastor these churches may become frustrated by the unwillingness of these congregations to move on to the future. The modest size of the congregation prohibits the pastor from receiving a living wage, so the pastor of a family church is often bivocational. In some larger family churches, there may be an unpaid or low-paid associate working in the area of youth, education, or music. Family churches typically increase in size slowly (by births, adoptions, or marriages among current members) or not at all, but adding a volunteer or part-time associate may allow a willing family church to grow by cultivating areas of discipleship and evangelism.

Discipling Church

The discipling church encompasses 70 to 150 active congregants in worship. Discipling churches may have grown out of a family church because the members were growth-focused. Typically these churches are highly dependent upon the pastor to maintain order, vision, and spiritual direction. The congregation enjoys the personal touch of the pastor in pastoral care because the members are few enough for the senior pastor to know each one by name and need. The pastor is usually the regular Sunday preacher, the sole instructor of Bible studies, and the leader in prayer meetings.

Because conventional wisdom says that a congregation should have one full-time pastor for every 100 active members in the congregation, a discipling church is usually the smallest size church to call an associate pastor. A part-time associate pastor may be considered at the 150-person threshold. Associate pastors in this context may be positioned to be the primary minister for outreach and evangelism or for children and youth.

Discipling churches are primed to grow because these congregations have the critical mass to sustain a decent budget. Most discipling churches are able to pay a full-time pastor, who is also the administrative leader of the church, and possibly another support staff person. When the church begins to realize that the growth of the congregation is forcing the pastor to limit pastoral care or one-on-one ministry, *that* is the time to search for additional ministry leaders. As the congregation begins to approach the range of 140 to 150 active congregants, churches need to plan for an associate pastor. If the church does not have a plan, the pastor will burn out or the church will not seek to grow because the pastor cannot possibly attend to everyone's needs. Some discipling churches will hire an associate pastor even before the growth has happened because the members believe that new leaders are needed to support that growth.

Churches would be well advised to gather a long-range planning committee to work toward the goal of preparing the church for an associate pastor. (There is more information about planning for an associate in Appendix A.) An associate pastor would need to focus on the two to three areas of ministry that require leadership. Often newly ordained ministers are picked for this type of church. This leaves the senior pastor more time to attend to pastoral care, visioning, coordinating committees, and administration.

Program Church

The program church is a church that has been able to grow beyond the size of the discipling church. The number of congregants attending worship service(s) in this church ranges from 150 to 300. Program churches have a high level of activity through ministry programs that involve both church staff and volunteer leaders. In such congregations, members of the laity are usually needed in key positions to drive and sustain programs. Organization in these churches is critical and often requires part-time or full-time staff persons. Thus, the program church typically has one or more paid associates.

The senior pastor spends a great deal of time training and supporting the leaders in critical ministry areas. An associate in this type of church is often a key player in the life of the church and plays a greater role in worship. Often the associate shares in some of the pastoral care and is expected to attend major and minor functions of the congregation. While the senior pastor is generally the primary preacher, he or she will also give opportunities to the associate(s) to preach at regular intervals during the year (e.g., four to six times).

For all these reasons, the senior pastor of a program church is well advised to develop a strong relationship with the associate pastor so that the church benefits from coordinated leadership. This is especially true because program churches need to have a strong sense of direction and vision around which they develop their ministry efforts. Associates will need to support that vision. Senior pastors should have transparent and frequent conversations with the associate about the vision of the church. In turn, the associate should be encouraged to exercise some freedom within achieving that vision.

Associates in program churches are usually generic or multi-purposed. While a seminary-trained associate is the normative choice for an associate in this church, those without seminary training may minister at program churches. Very few churches at this level have an associate working in just one ministry area such as youth or education. Associates in this type of church also oversee several lay members or staff persons who direct specific ministries in the church. The associate may even hold separate meetings, aside from the weekly staff meetings, that incorporate only the ministries for which the associate is responsible. Rarely would the senior pastor be present at these meetings. Much of the direction and administration that the senior pastor provides would involve frequent staff meetings.

Corporate Church
Corporate churches are so categorized because of their size, complexity, professionalism, and large staff. These churches embrace 300 to 800 active worship attendees and have an

extremely visible and vibrant ministry in the community. These churches are known for their internal ministry programs and their outreach initiatives in their town or city.

Because of its size, the corporate church requires several associate pastors. Music and worship are usually crucial components in these churches and most likely have a full-time paid associate pastor leading much of the music and worship ministry. A youth minister is another common staff position, and typically some sort of education or administrative associate is present to oversee the day-to-day operations of the church. Especially in larger congregations, a pastoral care associate serves in at least a part-time role.

Because the senior pastor in a corporate church is a charismatic and public figure, highly successful at organization and staff development, much of the interaction with church members is conducted by the associate pastors. Pastoral care visits may be solely handled by associate pastors or even lay leaders such as a board of deacons or elders. At the corporate church level, each associate pastor routinely cares for 100 to 150 people with whom he or she is involved on a weekly basis.

The associates are positioned to work well together as a leadership team and usually hold ministry degrees at the undergraduate or graduate level. Strong intrapersonal skills are needed from associates to create successful ministries where people are able to connect to the larger life of the congregation. Associate pastors lead in major areas of the church and teach in Bible studies, have a voice in congregational meetings, and make decisions that affect the ministry of the church. This is all guided by the senior pastor, but significant autonomy is given to the associates. These associates are often already established in their calling and desire to focus on their specialized ministry area. The senior pastor is able to use the diverse gifts of each associate to achieve and support the vision and function of the church's ministry.

Megachurch

The term "megachurch" is a popular one that reflects a large, almost city-sized congregation. Megachurch status has been highly prized, but just 2 to 3 percent of all congregations fall within this category. That number is rising, however. Since the 1970s, the number of megachurches grew from one to two hundred to thousands of megachurches in just about every tradition and denomination of Christendom—although some of the largest and best known are independent of any denomination, such as Saddleback Church, Willow Creek Community Church, and Lakewood Church. (For this reason, a number of church researchers believe that megachurches act as a congregational drain on smaller mainline churches.)

While eight hundred or more active members qualify a congregation for megachurch status, the most famous megachurches have thousands of active congregants. Church staffs at these congregations swell with associate pastors, ministry directors, program coordinators, church administrators, assistants, and interns. These large churches need associate pastors to oversee vast budgets, a number of staff people, and lay leaders. Indeed, associate pastors in the megachurch often minister to the same number of total people found in a program church, becoming almost senior pastors in their ministry specialty or geographic community.

These churches may have a teaching associate who preaches in the major worship services and an administrative associate who oversees the daily functions of the church. Associate pastors in megachurches may preach monthly because of the number of worship services on Sunday mornings, Saturday evenings, and during the week. Megachurches may provide several outreaches to the greater community by offering a Christian school, a bookstore, after-school programs, or a community center. In this way, they function almost as mini-cities, and associate pastors run major aspects of this city.

Because many megachurches are nondenominational, the educational requirements for associate pastors vary. Typically, mainline churches require all clergy to have a seminary degree. In some megachurches, associates may have doctorates, but in others, the associate pastors may have no higher education. Megachurches tend to need specific associates. For instance, associate pastors in these churches may have recreational ministries that compete with town or city sports programs. How many churches can boast of their sports program?

Searching for Associates

Some churches in search of an associate pastor may choose to initiate the typical search-and-call process, wherein a position is created by the church and the church uses denominational resources or advertises the opening in print or online. Most mainline denominations have a process or system that creates clergy profiles or résumés for individuals who are looking for pastoral work; such systems also allow a church to create a profile listing that helps denominational leaders place a new minister. These systems may be used for associate pastor positions as well as senior pastorates. In congregational traditions where each local church is autonomous, a search committee is typically responsible for seeking a new minister and will hire an associate with congregational approval.

The associate doing his or her own search for a church placement may turn to denominational resources, ministerial networks, and classified advertisements online or in print. Many congregations will post job openings on their websites, and any Internet search engine will produce a number of hits. Many ministry websites offer their services (some fee-based, others free of charge) to post position openings or résumés. Secular websites and job hunting services should not be overlooked. Churches have been known to post associate pastor openings on corporate job websites and in newspapers. Social media tools are increasingly valuable in vocational searches. Facebook, Twitter, Google+, and LinkedIn are social networking sites that can connect churches with potential associates looking for a church to serve.

The Internet isn't just for networking either. Many churches and denominational leaders have discovered the value of using video conference services such as Skype or GoTo Meeting to interview candidates without incurring the expense of flying candidates across the country. Those churches in search of high-caliber candidates not only may post their job opening on their website but also will want to register their site with a major search engine.

Tech-savvy ministers may create a website devoted to displaying their gifts of ministry. Clergy candidates may also choose to develop a high-quality blog (updated at least weekly) that shares insights about who they are, what they believe, and their philosophy of ministry. Posting sermon manuscripts, Bible study outlines, and entries relating to pastoral care, devotional reflection, and practical ministry matters may provide seeking congregations with a window into the aspiring associate's communication skills, vocational passions, and theological doctrine. These online tools can quickly identify serious candidates.

If churches do not have a clue what a "good" associate looks like on paper, then church leaders might want to consult with ministerial colleagues from neighborhood churches or other congregations in their denomination or association. What do other churches look for in an associate pastor? What experiences have other congregations had with fresh-from-seminary ministers versus career associates, with bivocational versus part-time associates? Calling up another senior pastor and asking about the role of his or her church's associates can help a search committee formulate what it is looking for in a candidate. Search committees can also browse other church websites to look at a church's staff page for the biographies of associate pastors. What is the educational background or ministry experience of other associate ministers of music or education or youth?

Christian colleges and seminaries have career offices that can put churches in touch with specific graduating students searching for associate pastor roles. Start with their music, education, youth, and counseling departments. Many will have a process by which the department chair connects local churches to graduating seniors for interviews. Some denominational offices hold face-to-face events for churches searching for pastors and for ministers searching for a church. At such events, search committees can conduct several interviews in one day, making the day productive and effective for churches and clergy alike.

Denominational Differences

The process of identifying and utilizing associate pastors differs from denomination to denomination. Most congregational churches (e.g., Baptist, Presbyterian, Pentecostal, Mennonite, nondenominational) use the search-and-call process. In connectional or semi-connectional churches (e.g., Methodist, Lutheran, Episcopal, African Methodist Episcopal, Church of God in Christ), denominational leaders usually appoint or help place associate pastors. These connectional congregations do have some say in what they want in an associate.

For example, I was hired as an associate pastor at a United Methodist congregation through a search-and-call process even though I was ordained as an American Baptist. This was an unusual situation, but the United Methodist Church's polity allows for ministers from other denominations to be used as full clergy in parishes of the United Methodist Church instead of the normative bishop-appointed pastor. The local church was searching for a particular kind of associate, and the leaders felt that they should consider candidates from a wider pool than just the United Methodist Church.

During my years with the UMC, I learned that bishops and superintendents work together to evaluate an associate's gifts and skills before appointing the associate to a senior or lead pastor role. Some United Methodist associate pastors remain associates for a decade or two before eventually moving into a senior pastorate. There was a time in the life of Methodist churches when clergy were moved or promoted every two years. The thought was that the church should experience the great talents of many pastors. Over the years, however, denominational leaders learned that longer pastorates are usually beneficial for congregations and for the minister's family. Similarly, in connectional churches, denominational leaders are learning that associate pastors cannot be treated as pawns in a career game of chess, in which one pastor can be moved for the benefit of another pastor.

Baptist groups, such as the American Baptist Churches USA, the National Baptist Convention USA, Inc., and the Southern Baptist Convention, may experience different rates of tenure of associate pastors. Because congregations in the free-church tradition have the responsibility of calling pastors, associate pastors in Baptist churches may move more freely and frequently—for better or worse. Certainly, God calls ministers to a particular church, but an associate may not be listening for God's leading in staying or going. In other Baptist churches, associate ministers are hired and fired at the will of the senior pastor. With this unhealthy model of leadership, a church may experience several associates in a brief time because the senior pastor is too demanding or dictatorial. Every church should have a staff relations committee that works as the human resources department of a church to help with conflicts, transitions, and oversight of church staff.

Almost every denomination has prized churches that offer the best opportunities, and every clergy member is vying for the opportunity to get their foot in the door. Some associates may want to "climb the ladder" and jump to a larger church where they may enjoy a higher salary or a more visible role in the congregation. Other associates do not have such ambitious aspirations but move from church to church in order to gain résumé experience, for personal enrichment, or for spiritual growth. Often when an associate pastor begins at a new church, congregants will ask questions such as:

> "How long will you be here? The last associate didn't stay too long."
> "Do you want to have your own church? I really don't like the senior pastor's preaching, but I like your preaching. I'll go to your church when you get promoted."
> "Are you going to become the senior pastor here? I just want to know because I don't think you have the right stuff to run this church."
> "Is this church just a stepping stone to another bigger church?"

Associate pastors should respond to these questions with answers that remind congregants that serving a church is a call from God. If associates give specific answers to these questions, it may cause unnecessary anxiety among church members. Moreover, some congregants can be brutally honest or downright mean. Avoid the temptation of badmouthing the senior pastor or sharing your career ambitions. Participating in this type of activity will make your tenure short and will undermine the pastoral leaders.

Whether a denominational leader or a search committee does the decision making, God is working through people to place pastors in the church where they are needed the most. Acts 2 testifies to this aspect of God's character. Jews were gathered from all over the known world for Pentecost and witnessed the power of God through the apostles. The Pentecost event was a lesson to those gathered that God was in control. Peter arose to explain that the revelation of the Holy Spirit to all people was what the prophet Joel foretold of. In other words, God had ordained the day of Pentecost to assist the early church. God worked through the leadership of the disciples to give God's people what they needed the most: the Advocate who would guide and empower the people for ministry.

Discovering Nontraditional Associate Work
Though churches would be duly served by a full-time paid associate pastor, this may not be possible. For congregations that think they cannot afford an associate pastor, some church polity does allow for unpaid or part-time associate pastors to minister in the church. For instance, connectional churches often hire outside of their denomination ministers who carry the title of "parish associate" or "ecumenical minister." This allows a church to hire a nontraditional associate pastor to do ministerial work without having to go through denominational requirements for education, pay, or ordination credentialing. These parish associates are able to perform many of the non-sacerdotal functions (e.g., preaching, teaching, visitation, but not baptism or Communion). Hiring a part-time parish associate has many benefits. A church receives the blessing of having another minister on staff without having to support a full-time salaried person. In addition, churches are able to have a trained associate pastor offer skills and gifts that might not otherwise be used because of denominational differences. Many ministers are willing to serve in churches with differing traditions.

Though it is not ideal, unpaid associate ministry is a reality in many churches. There may be a long denominational tradition that only the senior pastor receives compensation. Other churches cannot afford to pay other pastors, so those congregations may want to consider asking retirees or seminary students to assume a staff role on a volunteer basis. Often these unpaid associates provide important skills in the areas of youth ministry, pastoral care, or education. The downside of this is that some congregations come to assume that associates do not expect or require compensation, and therefore it may be difficult to break the pattern of having unpaid associates.

Discussion Questions for Churches

1. What type of church are you? (Please refer to the descriptions in this chapter: house, family, discipling, program, corporate, mega.)

2. What type of church do you want to become? Why?

3. How can an associate pastor help you in becoming the church you want to be?

4. What can be done to help limit hurtful comments from congregation members to associates?

5. How can the senior pastor better place associates in the life of the congregation?

6. What type of work would you like to see your associate doing in one, three, and five years?

7. How can your denomination, region, or association help you find an associate pastor?

8. Have you considered unpaid or nontraditional associates? Why or why not?

9. What community needs are present? How can an associate address those needs?

10. In searching for an associate, to what extent did you use online resources? Who in your congregation can help you find online resources for recruiting or searching for an associate pastor?

Discussion Questions for Associates

1. What type of church do you serve in? Please refer to the descriptions in this chapter.

2. How does your work contribute to the success of the larger congregation?

3. What areas in your congregation need attention?

4. How do your currently involve yourself in those areas? If you are not currently involved, how could you involve yourself?

5. What can you do to better communicate your ministry gifts?

6. Have you ever considered nontraditional associate work or unpaid associate work? Why or why not? What makes this type of work appealing?

7. How can you better highlight your ministry gifts?

8. See the ministry case study in Appendix C and consider the questions for reflection.

PART THREE

The Challenges and Opportunities
of the Associate Pastor

CHAPTER 6

What Makes Working as an Associate Pastor Risky?

A number of years ago, I was interviewed on the phone for an associate pastor position that would be half-time youth minister and half-time general associate. The church was a medium-sized congregation that had been in existence for about fifty years and had approximately 350 members. The senior pastor went on about the work, and he lamented that he was tired of associates who "played around." I was not sure what he meant by that, so I asked him.

He responded, "You know. The type of associate that does not stay around long, wants to move up the ladder, and does not pay the rent."

"Pay the rent?" I asked.

"Yes, pay the rent. Doing those jobs that the other pastors do not want," the senior pastor said flippantly. I took as long as I could to compose my thoughts without creating an awkward pause in the phone conversation. Finally I gulped and said my piece: "I'm not in the ministry to 'pay the rent.' That just sounds like you are doing something reluctantly. I'm not interested in paying the rent."

Let's face it. Working as an associate pastor is not glamorous. You are not preaching every Sunday, your name is not on the church sign, you get paid less or not at all, and many church members (and leaders) assume you are leaving soon anyway. Of course, it is to be hoped that none of us go into ministry for the name recognition and position of authority; we should be in ministry because God has called us to serve God's people. An associate *is* paid less than his or her senior pastor, and as in most supervisory relationships, working with a senior pastor may be challenging. Some senior pastors have been solo pastors for so long that they tend to micromanage a new associate; others will establish a power-based relationship with other ministers on staff and minimize or exploit those who might otherwise be clergy partners.

For all these reasons and more, it may not be surprising that church members who assume you aren't long for this position are proven right. The typical tenure of an associate pastor at a church is two to three years. If you remain in a position beyond three years, you have outlasted most associate pastors.

Associates often voice concerns that come from a position of frustration. One associate put it this way:

> Our senior pastor struggled with how to manage such a large staff. He was extremely effective on all of the general pastoral elements, but he struggled with matching both vision and leadership. He had never served a church this size, was very near retirement, and self-admitted that he avoided conflict—a perfect storm for the status quo. Therefore, our staff were very self-motivated but not united in their ministry goals. This dynamic made it difficult to retain high-capacity staff and often morale suffered.

Some associates experience good and bad times during their pastorate. Another associate expressed this give-and-take:

> Our staff dynamics have had some tension but also work well together. We don't do enough regular stuff

together. Even when we go to birthday lunches, we talk about work, but we are trying to be better about this. I think much of staff dynamics are unique in each place. The similar component necessary in each church is to learn what works for you. Listen to one another, and remember who you are all really working for.

Being flexible with the tension in multi-pastor staff situations is critical for the associate pastor. While you should have the freedom to express your joys and concerns, the concerns should be shared privately with the senior pastor. Recognize now that you are not going to get your way every time. Also understand that being an associate can be risky work.

The Risks of Associate Ministry

Two types of risk exist in associate ministry. The first type of risks are good risks. What are good risks? Good risks are those situations where new ideas can be fostered and acted upon. For example, an associate in a transitional neighborhood sees a large immigrant community in need of basic necessities and employment assistance. The church has a budget of $5,000 for outreach. The associate uses that money to start a program of assistance, job training, job placement, and a food pantry. The church is anxious about this new ministry, but the senior pastor lets the associate run with the idea. Will the associate be able to show real measureable outcomes for spending $5,000 on an assistance program ?

The second type of risk is one that damages the longevity of the associate's tenure or relationship with the senior pastor, staff, congregants, or community. If an associate pastor is to have any longevity or fruitful ministry, he or she should watch for these five risks to associate pastor ministry: burnout, being "all things to all people," staff, conflict, micromanagement, and trying to outshine.

Burnout

This risk is common for every minister, but especially for associate pastors. If a church grows large enough to have a second pastor it is common for that associate to become the "catch-all" minister. Juggling meetings, youth group, Sunday school, the occupational hospital visit, last-minute projects, and planning for a children's ministry event can overload an associate. Sometimes, the nature of not having a focus in parish work can cause burnout in associates. That is why churches and staff relations committees should have a well-defined summary of duties or a position description for associates (see Appendix B). Having specific boundaries of what is and is not included in the associate's job will help the church's ministry. Burnout occurs when associates feel that their work is not valued or recognized. Sometimes intense pressure from the senior pastor or church can cause burnout.

Balancing all areas of an associate pastor's life is challenging. When asked how one associate balances her ministry and personal life, she replied:

> I wish I had that figured out! I find this issue to be incredibly challenging. I love having time to myself at home in the mornings, so I made the decision not to go into the office until 10:00 on most mornings. I use my morning time to go to the gym, walk the dog, do some reading, eat a leisurely breakfast, etc. I am also very intentional about taking a day off each week and I do take all my vacation and continuing education time. There are many weeks during the program year when I am at the church on Tuesday, Wednesday, and Thursday evenings, which is not a good practice. I miss seeing my spouse! But I do the best that I can and try and give myself some grace when I feel like I'm not doing a great job of this whole "balance" thing.

Working too much at church and taking on too many tasks can lead to burnout. The feelings of burnout include apathy toward problems in the church, feeling hopeless, lack of motivation, feeling numb, exhaustion, lack of sleep, weight gain or weight loss, dependence on drugs or alcohol, depression, feeling like you do not have enough time to perform important tasks, and feeling like nothing you do is appreciated. At some point in church work, one or two of these feelings will occur, but if you have experienced all of these feelings, chances are that you are burned out.

Feeling stressed and experiencing burnout are two different things. Everyone experiences stress, but if that stress overtakes your life, health, relationships outside of church, and your psychological well-being, it is a recipe for disaster. Just read this story of an associate pastor when asked about how to handle the stress of associate ministry:

> Not very well, I am afraid. I think there are swings in both directions. When something is happening in my personal life, it affects my ministry. When ministry isn't going well, I notice it in the fit of my clothes. Our lives are not compartmentalized, nor should they be. However, taking time to recharge is important. The only other thing I would say that is unique in associate role for self-care is the identity crisis that sometimes goes on in my head. I was a solo pastor before being an associate. Sometimes I still act like a solo pastor even though I am working with a team. One way I remember that my current job does not dictate who I have always been is by maintaining long-term friendships and close ties with other clergy.

The key to dealing with burnout is first to recognize burnout. However, we usually do not notice those signs creeping into our life until we are overwhelmed.

The good news about burnout is that it can be reversed. This is where we seek out a third party to help us. This should be a trusted friend or mentor who is not a member of the congregation. You may also seek out a group of other associates or professionals with whom you can meet regularly to blow off steam or work through stress. Usually, a group of other associates or care professionals can help identify problem areas and suggest healthy practices of work, play, and family life. Seeing a counselor is another choice. In some extreme cases of burnout, more long-term therapy may be needed to undo the harm caused by burnout.

Another vital step in reversing the effects of burnout is taking care of your body. The emotional and physical toll of burnout can lead to series heath concerns. Getting more exercise and eating right can change the effects of burnout. Establish a pattern for your day and week that leads to more stability (see chapter 8). Learn to take vacations or breaks so that you are rested emotionally from your work.

"All Things to All People"

Scripture interpretation is challenging, but one particular passage of Scripture has led many associates to feel frustrated about or even despise their work. Since associates usually do all types of ministry work, associates feel pulled from every direction. Paul wrote to the Corinthians, "I have become all things to all people, that I might by all means save some" (1 Corinthians 9:22). Many ministers have used that verse to justify overworking their staff or to explain a need to be everything to everyone. How many families have suffered a pastor working sixty, seventy, or eighty hours a week because pastors feel that they must be all things to all people? The problem with this Scripture is that Paul was not communicating that he agreed to every demand, and therefore, we must say yes to every demand. To put this Scripture in context, we must understand the wider picture of Paul what was writing about:

To the Jews I became as a Jew, in order to win Jews. To those under the law I became as one under the law (though I myself am not under the law) so that I might win those under the law. To those outside the law I became as one outside the law (though I am not free from God's law but am under Christ's law) so that I might win those outside the law. To the weak I became weak, so that I might win the weak. I have become all things to all people, that I might by all means save some. I do it all for the sake of the gospel, so that I may share in its blessings.

Do you not know that in a race the runners all compete, but only one receives the prize? Run in such a way that you may win it. Athletes exercise self-control in all things; they do it to receive a perishable wreath, but we an imperishable one (1 Corinthians 9:20-27).

Here, Paul writes about the challenge of reaching people for Christ. That is, he must share the same gospel message to Jews, Gentiles, slaves, or free peoples. Paul was savvy about his outreach. He was able to use his upbringing in Judaism to communicate the gospel to the Jewish people. As a Roman citizen, he was able to speak about Jesus in terms that Gentiles would know. He did all of this, as he states, "that I might by all means save some." The apostle adapted his teaching so that particular groups of people could understand his message, yet without compromising the core of the message. Paul goes on to write about the self-discipline of athletes. The best athletes are able to balance diet, training, skill, and strategy to win the prize. Athletes must stay focused. Likewise, associates must be able to adapt to changing situations in order to do their work. However, if the athlete said yes to every demand, then the athlete would not be able to train and win the race. Likewise, the associate cannot say yes to every demand or be everything to everyone. No one can do that! Who can be a boss, a parent, a best friend, and a pastor to someone? Those are too many roles that cross too many boundaries.

Associate pastors need to learn the skills of balancing their time at church and at home. Associates need to learn that people will be disappointed if you cannot leave your daughter's birthday party to come and counsel a couple's failing marriage. There is a time and a place for your daughter's birthday party. Likewise, there is a time to provide pastoral care for a couple's marital issues. Congregations need to be educated as well. Senior pastors and associates need to model good decision making. Churches should learn that their pastor is not a 24/7 concierge service. Yes, senior and associate pastors can be called in the middle of the night if a church member is about to die and the family needs pastoral care. However, calling a pastor to come over on Christmas day to help clip coupons is a demand that should not made by church members.

Staff Conflict

Staff conflict is inevitable. The key to addressing staff conflict is responding. Chapter 4 dealt with understanding how conflict begins and thrives in the church and how to address it. Staff conflict often stems from insecurity. No matter the position in the church, staff can become insecure when faced with new leaders, roles, direction, routine, or personalities or with tension in the church. Staff members become anxious about their work and standing within the church. The key to dealing with staff conflict is not to feed it.

Consider this scenario: The church secretary just "had it out" with the senior pastor in a meeting where she told the pastor everything she was doing wrong. The church secretary wants to gossip with you about the "things she knows" concerning the senior pastor. If you stay and listen to the gossip, then you are feeding her desire to talk behind the pastor's back. Do not fall into the trap of being a silent coconspirator in the church secretary's plan to usurp the pastor's ministry.

Conversations that involve secrets within the staff lead only to hatred and animosity. Jesus said, "Blessed are the peacemakers," not "Blessed are whose who gossip." Associates are called to be peacemakers. The risk of becoming a participant in feeding staff conflict is very real. The risk of conflict will always be present; however, staff persons are called to be sources of trust and grace in times of tension. Be quick to listen and slow to speak, as Scripture directs. The associate who desires unity and is able to act upon that desire will be an asset to any senior pastor. Jason Byassee correctly articulates the theological role and gospel relationship that associate and senior pastors have:

> Relationships between associate and senior pastors are neither more nor less complicated than other human relationships: they hold the potential for abuse as well as for transformation. The gospel promises to transform human relationships as Jesus changes us from enemies to friends of God. Therefore any and all theological claims about relationships—about everything from sin to reconciliation and the eschatological summing-up of all things under Christ—are important to consider.[1]

Micromanagement

The definition of micromanagement is to manage or control with unwarranted attention to trivial details. This type of unhealthy behavior comes from a need to focus acutely on the process of a task rather than the results of a task. The risk of micromanagement is more for senior pastors than it is for associate pastors. Micromanagement does not usually occur because associate pastors are ineffective. What senior pastor wants to do an associate pastor's job? If an associate pastor is ineffective, he or she will most likely receive a request from the senior pastor to meet to discuss said failings.

I read a denomination's handbook on associate pastor ministry with regard to senior pastors, and I was shocked to see the following: "Don't make me micromanage." That is an excuse for a senior pastor to micromanage. Senior pastors do not want to waste time to micromanage an associate unless micromanagement fulfills a personal need to control or manipulate associate pastors. This need to control or oversee minute details comes from a senor pastor's emotional insecurity and is a behavior that begins long before an associate ever steps inside a church. Support staff and pastoral staff need to know that clear boundaries help to guard against such counterproductive behavior.

Associates can guard against micromanagement behavior in four ways.

Ask for all the information up front. Asking the senior pastor for all information about the church and asking as many questions as possible about the senior pastor will help guard against micromanagement. Associate pastors can also ask or volunteer for projects or assignments in which they will succeed. If your strength is not youth ministry, then do not ask to create a youth group event or lead youth on a retreat weekend. Communicating your progress on a project or a delegated task will help a senior pastor to know that she or he does not have to become a major presence in the task. If you do find that a senior pastor is micromanaging your work, ask questions:

> "Which decisions do you disagree with? Why?"
> "Which projects do you take issue with? How would you do those projects differently?
> "How could I work more efficiently with you?"
> "What do you value the most in ministry?"
> "How can I overcome these perceived failures?"

"How can we create a system for tracking goals met and
rating my progress?"
"In which five areas have I failed my job description?"
"How can we measure my progress forward toward
a shared goal?"

Work directly with the senior pastor. At the first sign of micro-management, do not run to the church's elders, deacons, or staff relations committee. Try to solve the conflict directly with the senior pastor. The ability to solve problems or conflicts on an associate's own power will speak volumes about the associate's personal boundaries and gifts as a minister. Sit down with the senior pastor face to face. Do not use email, phone messages, or a written note to express tension in the relationship. Set a time and a place where the two of your will not be interrupted. Come up with a plan to address the conflict and agree on terms that dictate when the conflict needs to be addressed in the future. Only when the senior pastor is unwilling to talk or address micromanagement should an associate pastor involve other church leaders. When other church leaders are brought in, keep the group as small as possible. If dozens of people sense there is tension among the pastoral staff, church leaders will become anxious. Feel free to talk with trusted colleagues or mentors who do not share a relationship with the church in any way.

Regularly spend time with the senior pastor. Building trust is the hallmark of any good relationship. Good marriages last for decades because of the love and trust that two spouses have for one another. The time spent together is what builds trust. The good times and the bad times establish a relationship that is grounded on experiences and is based on how a couple has bettered themselves because of these experiences. In many ways, associates and senior pastors are no different. Ministry partners must spend time together. Senior pastors should spend at least one hour a week meeting with the associate to talk about ministry in the church. Associates should also seek out the senior pastor for a regular lunch or coffee outing at least once a month where the two do not talk about anything related to the church. For larger staffs, this time away from church can be with several associates if needed.

An associate would do well to learn the interests, passions, and motivations of the senior pastor. Spending quality time is key. If possible, have the associate and the senior bring their families together. The first six months of an associate's relationship with a senior pastor can often make or break the associate's longevity. If regular patterns of time spent together are not established in those first six months, it is more likely that the senior and the associate pastor will not have a quality relationship. Associate and senior pastors need not be best friends, but they do need to have healthy boundaries of "togetherness" and individuality.

Keep the senior pastor informed but not overloaded. Associates should keep the senior pastor informed on a regular basis as to how the associates are doing in their specific ministry area, but the goal is not to overburden the senior pastor with laborious details. Too much information could include informing the senior pastor about mundane tasks, unrelated stories, or long descriptions of work accomplished. A good senior pastor will ask the right questions to keep informed. Too many details will bog down the time spent with the senior pastor and will take away from other important details such as growing areas, successes, and new people being reached.

If there are areas of concern, particularly when it comes to concerns about lay leaders, sharing details does become important. Associates should feel free to share danger spots. Danger spots are situations, relationships, or events with the potential for unhealthy behavior to begin or continue. For instance, if a youth pastor is meeting with a senior pastor about youth ministry and the youth pastor has some concerns about a male teenager and a female youth leader spending too much time together, that would be important danger spot that the senior pastor should know about.

Trying to Outshine

As an associate, knowing that you are not at the top of the church's organizational structure can be a difficult fact to accept. Competition between senior and associate pastors can develop quickly. Associate pastors need to know their role, but senior pastors should also not hinder an associate from becoming successful. Speaking publicly about a senior pastor in negative ways is a sure-fire way to a short associate pastorate. In some free-church traditions, it is a frequent occurrence that an associate who experiences a ministry of longevity can assume the role of a senior pastor within the same church. However, this change of role within a church is challenging. Several major conflicting realities will appear once the associate pastor becomes the senior pastor. The most evident reality will be the type of the relationship the former senior pastor and the former associate pastor (now senior pastor) had. Past differences and clashes could be made public, which leads church leaders to manage the damage.

The risk here is for associates to think that they can outshine the senior pastor. Rev. Don Hanshew, formerly an associate pastor at Fountain City United Methodist Church in Knoxville, Tennessee, and now pastor of Holston View United Methodist Church in Weber City, Virginia, gives this guidance on understanding resentment:

> There are some very real temptations as an associate pastor. Number one, pride. You have to keep the ultimate goal in mind and not get your feathers all worked up when other staff re-invent your ideas and concepts as their original ideas. Instead, take this as a high form of

flattery and that your passions are being organically integrated into the larger community. Two, resentment. Get over that the senior clergy gets paid more than two times your salary, takes more time off, and is usually out of the office by 4 p.m. The antidote for resentment is compassion. Have compassion on the senior pastor and pray that when you are old, get tired easily, and struggle with deep internal questions of effectiveness you will not have some flippant associate pastor but one that has compassion and energy to invigorate you. Just like you are searching for new people who feel a call into ministry, you need to be aware of the pastors who have so much to offer but are just tired and need their passions flamed.

Understanding the role of the senior pastor is helpful. The senior pastor has different demands from an associate. Trying to undercut a senior pastor is wasted energy. All the energy that goes into thinking, dreaming, scheming, and drawing up a plan to outshine the senior pastor could have been spent on ministering effectively. Instead, that energy went to usurping the senior pastor. The genesis of trying to outshine a senior pastor could come from insecurity, the need for attention, or the need to be in control. Those patterns of behavior are damaging to churches and should be dealt with sooner rather than later in an associate's tenure. If need be, the associate may have to be asked to leave if the culture of the church becomes toxic with the associate's dysfunctions.

Collaboration with senior pastors can make or break an associate pastor's ministry. Keeping a focus in the associate's area is critical. Associates would be well advised to remember their calling and remember why God has anointed them to do the sacred work of ministering. Asa Lee, assistant pastor at Mount Olive Baptist Church in Arlington, Virginia, keeps this in mind with his advice:

Stay the course and be true to your calling. Working relationships with challenging senior pastors can be very frustrating and lead to the acting out of associates in a lot of negative ways, most of which are picked up on (or even encouraged) by members of the congregation. However, in those situations I have found it helpful to remember my own calling to ministry and do my best to complete the tasks in front of me. Some pastors are just difficult people to work with, others are very distrustful of associates and approach working with them skeptically. In either case, the way to combat this is to do the job assigned. In remembering your calling to the work of ministry, you never lose sight of your *real* function in ministry and the role God has assigned for you. As much as you can stand it, never act out and never subvert the authority of your senior pastor. This always affects your credibility with the congregation as well as with future assignments.

Acting out is usually a symptom of a deeper emotional issue. Like a child looking for attention, an associate pastor may choose to respond by undercutting the senior pastor behind closed doors or even in public arenas. No matter how offended an associate pastor feels, sabotage is never a healthy course for anyone.

The responsibility of senior pastors is enormous. Overseeing or guiding associates, staff, and volunteers can be very demanding. Senior pastors also stay focused with vision, mission, ministry direction, budgets, worship, spiritual direction, and pastoral care of the church. Being able to keep all this in motion requires good administrative skills and spiritual strength. Associates need to know that they are part of the system of a church. In addition, senior pastors need to know that associates are an important part in that system. Associates are not junior pastors who can be manipulated like a marionette by a puppet master who pulls strings to make the associate move at will. There is mutuality but there is also the understanding that the senior pastor has the final say in major decisions. If senior pastors get involved with micro-managing an associate's decisions, then it only spells disaster for the senior-associate relationship and the church. Seniors need to give associates chances to grow in ministry and to schedule their time effectively. Osaze Murray, who served in several associate pastor positions in Baptist churches in Virginia and Philadelphia, Pennsylvania, offers some thoughts:

> My advice for senior pastors supervising associate pastors is to provide as many opportunities for associate pastors to serve in pastoral roles as possible, after which provide them feedback (what was done well, how they might improve, etc.). Another advice would be to help associate pastors review their schedules twice a year. Now, when I say help them with their schedules what I mean is help them to know that it's okay to read the Word or pray for two hours or it's okay to get tea with your wife one morning. I personally struggle with some of the liberties of an open schedule because I'm not always aware of how others use their time. So I think helping to review the schedule is appropriate and would be a big help for associates.

Senior pastors should see themselves as encouragers and not correctors. Encouraging associate pastors to do their best work will produce the best results. Senior pastors should not interfere in the process if the associate is succeeding in the goals set forth by the church or pastoral/staff relations committee. Often, many senior pastors spend a good portion of their time with associates correcting what senior pastors see as mistakes or missteps. Both senior and associate pastors can benefit from remembering four ideas that will mutually benefit both types of pastors.

Always remain teachable. Jesus commissioned his followers to make disciples of all nations (Matthew 28). The process of making disciples is called discipleship. Discipleship is a lifelong process because attuning one's self to the teachings of Scripture takes a lifetime if not more. The reason why discipleship is a lifelong process centers on the fact that learning is a lifelong process. We keep learning because our brains are structured that way. The expression, "You cannot teach an old dog new tricks" is often used as a excuse for not learning new processes or information. For both the associate and senior to always remain teachable gives everyone equal responsibility for learning. It is arrogant to think that a fifty-eight-year-old pastor cannot learn anything from a twenty-five-year-old associate pastor. A wise senior pastor would see the new associate as someone who could be clued into cultural changes and new social undercurrents. The younger pastor may also have skills in newer technologies, strategies, or approaches to ministry.

Likewise, the associate should keep an open ear to what a senior pastor has learned about congregational practices, leadership, and healthy ways of balancing the demands of church and a pastor's family life. An associate coming from seminary or from the business world may have just as much to offer as a senior pastor with twenty years of pastoral experience. The key to unlocking the knowledge is to take a posture of openness and acceptance of each other's gifts, strengths, experience, and education. The lines of communication will break down when one person in the senior/associate relationship believes that he or she has nothing more to learn.

Look for unconventional sources for new insights. Smart ministry leaders know that they may not have all the ideas or answers to a solution. Any pastor or staff should realize a good idea when they see it. It does not have to be your own idea, but credit should be given to the originator. Both senior and associate pastors should utilize unconventional sources for new ideas and possible solutions to problems. Conferences, books, and ministry websites have good resources for best ministry practices, but pastors should also look elsewhere. Taking an idea from the secular world is a start. Companies like Google and Microsoft allow their employees to use a certain percentage of their time on work-related personal projects. Even though employees are working on the company's time clock, the creativity used on the personal project related to their work will help create solutions to work-related tasks and projects. This is an unconventional solution to a conventional problem: How can employees become more creative?

Pastors can take this unconventional idea from a non-ministry setting and apply it to the church. Senior pastors could allow their associates to work on personal ministry projects during their work week to help associates with new ideas. For example, allowing pastors to work on blogs, articles for ministry publications, curriculum, creative arts, or music could enable them to use their gifts to help an area of ministry in the church. Taking a cue from the secular world can help pastors use their gifts in unconventional ways. Senior pastors need to broaden their horizons to include looking to unusual sources for ideas and solutions.

Always remember the big picture. Micromanagement is about details, or more accurately, getting caught up in details. It is about the need to control. Sometimes people cannot help themselves because they are focusing on the wrong goals. Senior pastors and associate pastors should focus on goals. Senior pastors need to give away a little control so that people can achieve results. Remembering that there are larger realities than process to a solution is the important. If the agreed result to a goal is to have five new small groups formed, then the staff or pastor responsible for that goal should have some freedom in achieving that goal. The only time a senior pastor needs to intervene in a process to a goal is if something went wrong, someone is being hurt, ethical standards are being ignored, or a dramatically dangerous situation arises. Associates should not see suggestions from senior pastors as intervening. Suggestions should always be welcomed with an attitude of open-mindedness and gratitude. Senior pastors should not feel offended when a suggestion is not taken. This leads us to the last point to keep in mind when senior pastors and associates are working together.

Let people fail. Failure is not a dirty word. Our culture has a problem with failure. We misunderstand failure. Failure can be a wakeup call to reality. Sometimes, we need a reality check. We need something to steer our course away from where we are heading. It can be difficult to realize that you have failed, but that is where failure helps. If associates or seniors spend time in self-loathing, then they can miss a great opportunity for growth because failure can lead to other opportunities.

A famous story illustrates how failure can lead to opportunity. While he was trying to invent a better battery, Thomas Edison's manufacturing facilities in New Jersey were leveled by fire in 1914. Edison lost almost a million dollars' worth of equipment and much of his research. The next day while walking around his burned-down facility, he said, "There is value in disaster. All our mistakes are burned up. Now we can start anew." Three weeks later he invented the phonograph, which in turned led to recording devices like tape players, CD players, and even digital music players, which were invented decades later.

If pastors seek failure as a teaching tool, then failure can be used to better one's ministry instead of destroying it. When pastors face failure, they have two choices. One is to crumble inside and never take a chance again. Or they can let God shape a pastor's ministry. Associates and senior pastors can encourage one another in the failures in ministry. Failures do not have to go down as blemishes on a record but as opportunities to try new directions.

Case Study: Connecting with Congregants

An Invitation to Speak

Cindy was asked to speak at the annual fall dessert of the women's club in her church. To prepare for the event, Cindy asked the club's president what she would be talking about. The president replied that each year a different staff member is asked to speak. Cindy thought it would boring to hear someone talk about herself, especially because the majority of these women knew her as a young, unpaid associate pastor.

At the dessert, Cindy saw a man who pastors a deaf church in the community. Cindy was unsure how many women would be at the function, so she sat by herself, but a church member whom she knew came over to sit with her. They talked for a few minutes, and then the evening's program began. The women discussed their plans for the upcoming year. Next, the pastor of the deaf church spoke about his ministry and performed an interpretive song for the deaf, which involved music, dance, and sign language.

After the pastor spoke, Cindy introduced her ministry and what she does in the church. She also shared Scripture and related her call to ministry to every Christian's call to be a servant of Christ. Cindy even joked about how the women did not know that they were going to get a sermon.

Learning from the Experience

At first, Cindy was afraid of the opportunity; she had even thought of backing out. Cindy had not decided what to talk about until five minutes before the dessert. She felt nervous because she did not know how to relate to forty women between the ages of forty and eighty-five. She felt insecure because she felt her ministry would not interest the group, and how was she going to be engaging after the talk given by the pastor of the deaf church?

To her surprise, Cindy found that she was engaging. Almost every woman thanked her for sharing. The women remarked that it was uplifting to know that young people are involved in ministry and church. Cindy also met many church members she had not met before.

Members of the women's club work together to help other ministries in the area. They volunteer at soup kitchens, homeless shelters, and homes for battered women. Cindy felt that as the only staff member present, she should try to find commonality with the older women. She also felt led to talk about her call. Cindy discovered that through talking about her own doubts, many women were able to connect with her ministry. She discovered that there are times when feeling led to talk about one thing is the right approach.

After the event, Cindy learned that most congregants want to know more about their associate's life, call to ministry, and how the associate came to the church. Church members truly wish to fellowship with the staff. Cindy, though a guarded person, discovered that there is appropriate information to share about one's life, and that she could share personal information. Cindy decided that she should spend more time with congregants and seek to be more comfortable with sharing personal information.

Discussion Questions for Churches

1. In what ways have you prepared for an associate to have a successful ministry?
2. What signs of burnout have you observed in your associate?
3. What steps could be taken to reverse or prevent burnout?

4. How does the senior pastor seek to maintain healthy boundaries with associates?

5. How does the church allow the associate to voice proper concerns in the church?

6. Which risk from this chapter is the hardest for your church to address? Why?

7. What risk from this chapter are you dealing with now?

8. What resources are available for church staff to help deal with conflict?

9. How has the church hindered an associate's success? How has the church contributed to an associate's success?

10. How often does the senior pastor meet with an associate? How often does the senior pastor spend time with the associate outside of the church?

Discussion Questions for Associates

1. What is the most challenging part of preventing burnout?

2. How do you handle micromanagement? What steps have you taken in the past to address micromanagement?

3. Do you feel that you have to be "all things to all people"? Why and in what ways?

4. How can you begin to establish boundaries for your work and the senior pastor's work?

5. How often do you meet with other trusted clergy or ministry professionals? How have you opened yourself up to suggestions, guidance, and direction of those outside resources?

6. What encourages you about your work as an associate?

7. What challenges your work as an associate?

8. How do you handle criticism?

9. What are your frustrations about how the church views you and your ministry? How do you contribute to these frustrations? If you are considering a transition out of your current ministry, review Appendix D, "When to Stay, When to Leave."

10. What would help you cope with critical feedback from the church or your senior pastor?

NOTES
1. Jason Byassee, "Team Players: What Do Associate Pastors Want?" *Christian Century* 123, no. 2 (2006): 18–22.

CHAPTER 7

What Makes Working as an Associate Pastor Rewarding?

One of the most meaningful experiences I ever had as an associate was when I ministered to the youth of the congregation and community I served after several local teenagers were involved in a car accident. These young people were coming back from a Young Life event when their car veered off the road and hit a tree. Four of the youth sustained injuries, some major and others minor. One teenager died. (Neither drugs nor alcohol was a factor in the crash.) A large number of youth in the congregation were friends with those who had been involved in the car accident, and some had been present at the Young Life meeting. I heard about the accident the next morning when a parent called me to tell me about it.

Immediately, I called the Young Life leader because I had a relationship with him and his workers. He confirmed the details. I called the high school and talked to the assistant principal who was a friend. She told me that the head principal wanted me to come to the school and help with the crisis. This was a tight-knit town where everyone knew everyone else. The principal later told me that the whole day would not be an educational day, but rather a grieving one.

When I arrived at the school, I saw teenagers in the hallways, holding one another, crying, yelling, and struggling even to stand. I made my way to the main office, where a number of the youth who had been present at the Young Life meeting were gathered. As I looked around the room, I realized that I knew three of the stunned and sobbing teenagers and only one of them was connected with the church. I wondered where the other fifty students who attended the church were. After talking with the principal, we decided that we should have a vigil service in the high school stadium that night. Preparations were made with other pastors in town. As the morning continued, I walked the hallways looking for the youth who attended the church. Each time I saw one, he or she would ask, "What are you doing here?" Each time I would reply, "I'm here for you and for the whole school." Some of the encounters were jovial and others were sorrowful.

The day progressed, and I was contemplating my role in the ordeal. What could I do in a few hours? What ministry could be done in a public school? How could I respond to so much grief? Those questions swirled in my head as I walked the halls, watching young people struggling to make sense of what happened. The young man who had died in the car accident was well-known and well-liked. What meaning or fulfillment for ministry could come out of this tragedy?

The vigil, attended by several thousand people, was led entirely by pastors in the community. We offered prayer, reflection, humor, encouragement, and hope. It was remarkable to see so many people from the town gathered. The vigil was a way for the community to discover that life is precious. It was also an opportunity for the town to seek strength in itself. People from all walks of life, of different ethnicities, social classes, and ages, unified to grieve together and to comfort one another.

That day I saw the best of a community and the opportunity for an associate pastor to make a difference. I may not have solved all the theological questions regarding suffering and the problem of evil, but I was able to be present and to be a source of consolation. I was able to be pastor that day. I was able to feel that I was helping others seek comfort. Though the circum-

stances were difficult, I was able to use all my training, education, and experiences to aid a community in mourning. The
reward of the experience was that my calling as a shepherd and
an encourager was becoming a reality. Being a pastor is about
serving. Sometimes serving is difficult, but it is always a labor of
love. It is meaningful and fulfilling because God is ministering
through us.

Opportunities in Associate Ministry

Just as chapter 6 covered five risks of associate pastor ministry,
this chapter includes five opportunities of associate pastor ministry. Each risk of associate pastoral ministry can be countered by
seeking to discover these five opportunities.

Be Molded by a Mentor

Your senior pastor can serve as a valuable mentor in ministry. He
or she most likely has several years of experiences as the head of
a staff in a congregation. In other words, he or she has learned
the ropes. After mistakes and successes, most senior pastors
quickly realize how firmly they can press church members into
new leadership roles and how to identify the trouble spots in the
congregation. Learn everything you can from your senior pastor.

A mentoring relationship does not have to be an official one,
but mentoring recognizes that learning is critical to the success of
staff relationships. Rev. Shaun King, senior pastor of College
Park Baptist Church in Orlando, Florida, gives us the key to
unlocking a successful mentor-mentee relationship in ministry:

> A great measure of trust can be nurtured through inten-
> tional one-on-one dialogues. In our context, I meet with
> a different member of our ministerial staff each
> Thursday morning. We call these meetings "staff con-
> nections." We used to call them "check-ups" but I

thought that image sounded a bit clinical and certainly implied more of an "over-under" relationship than what I wanted. In our connections (which work out to be about one per month), we spend time talking about family and personal journey issues. Then we look at the associate's individual six-month and one-year goals to see what kind of progress is being made, and if necessary, we work through some of the hurdles and roadblocks together. It is also a time for them to express any concerns with me, which they may feel inhibited to share within the larger context of staff meetings.

Being able to sit down with the senior pastor on a regular basis can bring great success to an associate pastor. It is important for the senior pastor to be seen as a cheerleader instead of an overseer in this relationship. As mentor, the senior pastor should do everything possible to encourage an associate in his or her work, offering advice and affirmation as well as accountability in the associate's vocational development and goal setting. With such measures in place, a senior pastor is more apt to give an associate more autonomy in ministry. A pastor-staff relations team or committee can assist a senior pastor in tracking these goals.

Some associates think that their partnership with their senior pastor suffers from a lack of trust. Trust is essential in a quality mentor relationship. The associate and the senior pastor can have differing philosophies on ministry. These differences could be minor, but if major differences exist in the relationship, it may be time for that relationship to end. However, one of the ways that an associate can learn what to do in ministry is to learn what not to do. Watching how a senior pastor operates can help solidify or change an associate's ministry philosophy. Associates observing their senior pastor's ministry in preaching, teaching, and administration (whether poor or excellent) can be a valuable teaching lesson that is never taught in a classroom or seminary course.

New Ministries Can Take Shape

Associate pastors are often ideally positioned to begin new ministries in the church. Senior pastors are busy working with committees, planning worship, attending to hospital visits, and managing staff. Associate pastors often have a little more flexibility in their work, and they may have more time as well—time for creative thinking, planning, and implementing new programs or ministries.

Sometimes associate pastors generate new ministries out of their specialties in youth ministry, music, education, or other areas. Younger associates may have a vision for a high-tech ministry that makes the most of church or ministry-specific Facebook pages, websites, podcasts, blogs, Tweets, e-devotionals, or mobile phone apps. Associate pastors who speak the language of a new, increasingly wired and socially networked generation may find themselves involved in innovative ministry programs for the elusive eighteen- to thirty-five-year-old population. And because of their more flexible schedules, associates are able to spend time developing frequent online encounters with this highly interactive generation.

Associate pastors often flourish in their new ministry areas. Starting a food pantry or a new Wednesday study group can birth excitement in the congregation and community about what the church is doing. Most people who come looking to join a church want a congregation that offers many ways to be connected and to serve. A senior pastor who advises the staff to come up with new ideas can become a think tank. The church staff can kick around and test the ideas, and associates can be innovative and take more risks with trying new ideas. When a senior pastor spearheads a change, the response from church members may be hostile or fearful because they wonder if the new ministry signals a change in the church's overall vision and direction. But when an associate is the innovator, it seems less of a threat to the church's larger way of being. It is viewed as ancillary, value-added, and less of a threat to the status quo.

At the same time, these new ministries and programs can become the centerpiece of an associate's ministry. If the proper work and planning occur, it is possible for the associate's ministry centerpiece to become one of the church's most successful ministries.

Be Involved with People on an Intimate Level

Spending time with people is perhaps one of the most obvious requirements of ministry, but it is often one of the most forgotten. Preparing sermons, planning for seasonal church programs, administrating meetings, and executing church retreats can leave little time for counseling, visitation, and one-on-one quality interactions with congregants. Many pastors leave the personal aspect of ministry last on their to-do list. Therefore, senior pastors may assign more pastoral care duties to associates to lighten their own load.

This works out well in large part because most associates have many fewer administrative responsibilities in the church—and thus they have more flexibility in their work hours and work load. (The exception here is the associate pastor who is designated as the administrative pastor.) An associate may also have more time to take congregants out for coffee or lunch because they have a lighter level of responsibility than does the senior pastor. Associates who work in the areas of children, music, youth, education, and pastoral care naturally have more time designated to spend quality time with people. An associate pastor who works directly with small groups routinely spends time with the small-group leaders; such interaction is essential in order to manage and evaluate their strengths and areas that may need improvement. An associate pastor who oversees the music ministry most likely needs to meet with musicians and worship leaders on a regular basis, which in turn leads to a strong relationship with those leaders.

Specialized Ministry Gives Focus

Would you rather do many things in an average manner or a few things really well? Many senior and solo pastors often feel burned out if they have numerous responsibilities in the church. Many churches expect their senior or solo pastor to be Bible teacher, preacher, chaplain, financial planner, administrator, head of staff, prophet, and conflict manager. All those responsibilities can lead to a fragmented ministry where many things get done in a run-of-the-mill fashion. Having to balance a life and ministry is difficult for any pastor.

In this, there are distinct advantages for an associate pastor: one can focus on two or three areas of ministry and excel in those areas. Having such a focus will help a church determine what new responsibilities it can and cannot give to an associate pastor. If the associate pastor responsible for the education ministry is suddenly now charged with the music ministry, then that associate should be able to communicate with the church leaders that perhaps another leader is needed. Focusing an associate pastor on two or three areas of responsibility usually produces the best success. Indeed, in larger churches, one area of responsibility would be a best practice. For instance, in a thousand-member church an associate could be used for only discipleship. But in a hundred-member church, an associate pastor could take on more than one area of ministry. Enabling staff ministers to use their passions and gifts can produce a fruitful ministry environment whereby the church receives the benefits of an enthusiastic and focused pastor. Churches who hire associates should look for ministers who have special skills in other areas that would benefit the church.

Skills in law, medicine, organizational management, recreation, music, or financial planning could help center an associate's ministry. This is where second-career or bivocational ministers are greatly prized.

Grace from Mistakes

Congregations can be places of dysfunction, but churches can also be stations of grace. Learning in associate pastor ministry is a valuable tool for any associate who senses a future call into senior or solo pastor ministry. By "mistakes" I mean those missteps that are the inevitable byproduct of real-life ministry. A well-balanced and self-differentiated senior pastor will allow associate pastors a good amount of freedom to explore their passions, gifts, and strengths in ministry. Making mistakes in the associate pastor role can be a proving ground for ministry ideas. Trying new strategies in preaching that uses new forms of technology, using new resources for Bible study, using a new instrument in worship, changing the order of worship, using new spiritual disciplines, or forming mission teams could be met with success or failure. Associates who explore the edges of the congregation's comfort level are associates who discover the church's boundaries. For example, an associate pastor who wants to lead a new small-group ministry begins with a very spiritual book that is deemed too mystical for some church members. The associate is generally given a measure of grace to survey and reevaluate which resources the congregation is comfortable using. Learning from such mistakes can produce thriving results in the future.

Ministers who attempt innovative approaches to conventional problems are sometimes called mavericks. Mavericks are not outlaws, anti-team players, or wild people; rather, mavericks investigate alternative ideas. Congregations are usually more accepting of mavericks serving in the associate role, especially if the associate is one who passionately plans, articulates, and implements different ministry approaches.

Putting It All Together

Truly rewarding ministry is found in its quality. Growth and success can be measured in many ways, and the same is true for what we have described as the rewards of associate ministry. It is critically important to understand that ministry as an associate pastor is not just about "feeling good" after visiting someone in the hospital. Rather, the reward is found in accomplishing what God has called the associate to do. Certainly, associates can feel good about reaching people for Jesus Christ, but the reward is not ours to claim—it is God's.

Like the faithful servant in the parable (Matthew 25), we all want to hear the words, "Well done, my good and faithful servant." On a staff with several other ministers, unhealthy competition can arise from trying to outperform other ministers. The opportunities in ministry should be centered on occasions where associates can effectively support the church in its work and add to the value that the senior pastor brings to the ministry. The reward that comes from witnessing a transformation into the Christian life is found in watching someone connect to God through the local church. Indeed, seeing a new disciple be welcomed into the Christian community is an exciting and fulfilling experience. It is those moments where an associate can feel that God has used his or her ministry for the renewal of another. Younger associates may find fuller meaning in assuming their ministry identity when they finally find their focus in ministry. Career or professional associates spend years in college, seminary, internships, field education, training, and observation for ordination. The reward of finally accomplishing everything required for pastoral ministry is to be celebrated and

honored among senior pastors, other associate pastors, churches, and religious intuitions.

Case Studies: Gaining Experience
Mike: Learning from a Different Ministry Style

After spending many years in internships and part-time church
positions, Mike had attained a great deal of experience in several areas of ministry. Though music was his area of greatest
expertise, Mike excelled at preaching, teaching, pastoral care,
and organizational management. Several senior pastors had
mentored Mike, and he had enjoyed the guidance and support
they offered.

A church hired Mike as an associate pastor, and he was
ordained shortly after. Mike had several positive experiences as a
part-time associate minister, but this was his first full-time position
in a church. In the first few months of his full-time position, it was
clear to Mike that the senior pastor was well-liked, but there were
times when Mike noticed that the senior pastor offended a number of people in the church. Some of these people left the church,
but in a church of five hundred members, these departing members were quickly replaced with new members. From time to
time, Mike would come up with new ideas for worship, education, and children's ministries because he was considered to be a
general associate with many areas of responsibility.

Within a year, Mike observed the senior pastor using some
heavy-handed approaches to securing leaders in lay positions,
manipulating church members to perform office tasks, and
becoming angry with parishioners who questioned his methods.
Some of these behaviors filtered into how the senior pastor man-
aged the staff, including Mike. Rather than trying to fight these
long-established behaviors, Mike carefully observed how the
senior pastor operated and sought to minimize conflict with him.
It was difficult for Mike to relate to the senior pastor, but Mike's

ministry was giving him focus and a sense of fulfillment. After talking with a few mentors, Mike decided to stay in the church until he sensed that God was calling him somewhere else. Mike used this time in his ministry to reinforce what he learned before he came to his current church. It was clear that the church tolerated the senior pastor's behavior because he was able to supply results and growth in membership.

After three years, Mike sensed a call to solo pastor ministry and left his associate position to serve in a small inner-city church. Instead of seeing his ministry and struggles with the senior pastor as wasted time, Mike learned more about how to engage in healthy ministry by watching unhealthy ministry practices.

Sam: Growing in Ability

The senior pastor asked his part-time associate, Sam, to visit Mr. Long, a neighbor of a church member, at the local hospital. Hospital visitations were not Sam's specialty in ministry. He did not enjoy visiting people he did not know. However, Sam's pastor knew that if Sam was going to become an effective associate he would have to grow to accept hospital visits. Sam believed that he shared a healthy relationship with his senior pastor; thus Sam trusted this assignment.

As Sam neared the room, he prepared himself for an agonizing experience of visiting an unknown person in the hospital. As he approached the door of the room, Sam could see a man with a cast on his leg. With a sigh of longing to leave, Sam entered the room and met the man on the bed. "Hello, my name is Sam, and I'm here to visit you today. I'm a pastor from the church down the street." The man smiled and welcomed Sam. The associate listened to the patient's life story and learned that the man lived in the city. His wife had died ten years ago, and he lived alone. Then the patient said, "Well, an old timer like me has trouble every now and again. I fell and broke my leg walking down the stairs of my house. The doctor had to surgically repair the leg."

Sam looked down at his watch and realized that he had been there for thirty minutes, which he thought was too much time to spend with a stranger. Sam gently interrupted the man's story and said, "I really need to go because I have an appointment to keep. May I pray with you?" "Yes, please do," the man replied. Sam closed his eyes and began his prayer: "Lord of healing, we ask that you will be with Mr. Long and . . . " Sam felt the man tapping on his arm. Sam opened his eyes, and the man said politely, "Excuse me, but my name is Mr. Evans. Please keep praying." Sam immediately felt embarrassed but continued with his prayer. After the prayer, Sam said goodbye and left knowing that he would have to find Mr. Long.

As Sam left the room, a doctor was standing nearby. The doctor had heard Sam praying and assumed that he was Mr. Evans's pastor. Mr. Evans did not have any family left, the doctor told Sam, and medical tests showed that Mr. Evans had liver cancer. The cancer had spread to other organs, and it was likely that Mr. Evans had only months to live.

Sam was moved by his experience (even though he never found Mr. Long) and decided to visit Mr. Evans every day. Each time Sam visited the hospital the fear and anxiety of hospital visits lessened. Mr. Evans and Sam talked about life, Scripture, faith, sports, and local news. After several months, Mr. Evans passed away. Sam officiated at his funeral and spoke about his pastoral relationship with Mr. Evans. After the experience, Sam asked his senior pastor for more opportunities to do hospital visitation and found visitation to be a rewarding part of his ministry.

Discussion Questions for Churches

1. What opportunities exist for an associate to find reward or fulfillment in ministry?

2. Who is responsible for setting goals for associates in the church? How are those goals tracked?

3. Who is mentoring your associate? What role does that mentor play in the associate's ministry?

4. What new ministries could be started by an associate pastor? What resources are available for new ministries? How can the church make more resources reachable for the associate?

5. How do associates use technology in their ministry? How could technology be used in the church to reach ministry goals?

6. Does the church or senior pastor encourage the associate to spend one-on-one time with congregants? Why or why not? How much time should an associate spend with individual churchgoers?

7. What is the church or senior pastor doing that encourages an associate to have a ministry focus? Is the associate's ministry split in too many different areas? If so, how can the church begin to give the associate focus?

8. How much grace or room for failure do associates have in their ministry? How is the associate encouraged to take healthy risks in new ministry areas?

Discussion Questions for Associates

1. What gives you fulfillment in ministry? What do you find rewarding?

2. Who is your mentor? How much time do you spend with your mentor? What insights does your mentor give you?

3. How does your mentor encourage you to reach your ministry goals?

4. What is the one thing you need right now to make associate pastor ministry rewarding or more meaningful? What steps can you take to make your ministry more rewarding?

5. List the ways you use technology in ministry. How does your senior pastor or church encourage you to use technology? What ways can you improve in your use of technology to make your ministry more successful?

6. How much time do you portion in your week for one-on-one encounters with people in your ministry? Setting a personal goal with one-on-one interactions with church people can be helpful. What is a realistic goal for weekly personal meetings with parishioners?

7. In what ways do you seek to create new ministry ideas, events, programs, missions, studies, fellowship, and worship interactions?

8. What have you learned from your unsuccessful ministry endeavors?

PART FOUR

The Associate Pastor in Action

CHAPTER 8

The Life of an Associate Pastor

There is a changing and encouraging trend in pastoral ministry. Several decades ago, it was not uncommon to hear that pastors worked fifty, sixty, or even seventy hours a week with little pay, contrasting starkly with other professions requiring comparable education and skills. Within the last fifteen years, however, more and more churches are realizing that fifty-five to seventy hours of work cannot be the right model for pastors if churches want to retain their leaders for any length of time.

Most major mainline denominations (United Methodist Church, Presbyterian Church USA, Episcopal Church USA, Evangelical Lutheran Church of America, and American Baptist Churches USA) have either required minimum pay levels or recommended pay minimums for their clergy. In addition, most national church bodies have guidelines for pastors and churches of a healthy work schedule. Since these mainline denominations require graduate-level education of their clergy, they approach ministry from a position of professionalism. This means they often think of their pastor much like they think of their doctor, therapist, lawyer, or school teacher: they have regular office hours. In independent churches, however, ministry is often seen as a calling that requires a great deal of personal sacrifice; part of that sacrifice features ministers who overwork themselves for the good of the church. This latter approach is seen as some sort of spiritual model that lends to the idea that a minister is truly called because clearly no one would work a comparable secular job for so little pay. Therefore, ministers *must* be called by God to sacrifice the income they might otherwise earn.

Obviously, there will be seasons and circumstances when any pastor works more than forty to fifty hours a week, as is the case with most full-time salaried positions in any organization. The challenge arises when people in the church (many of whom enjoy forty-hour work weeks, healthy salaries, and full benefits) assume that their pastor will regularly work fifty-five hours or more for less compensation and inferior benefits. This is a recipe for disaster because it creates a toxic mix of injustice between pastors and church members. (See Appendix E for a healthier recipe for associate pastor compensation.)

It is impossible for a church to biblically justify such an expectation, yet too many congregations seem to believe that they must keep their pastors honest by keeping them poor. We read in 1 Timothy 5:18, "For the scripture says, 'Do not muzzle the ox while it is treading out the grain,' and 'The worker deserves his wages.'" In other words, do not shortchange the one who deserves compensation. Pastors burn out and leave ministry because of such little pay and benefits compared to their professional counterparts (e.g., hospital chaplains, counselors, social workers, and teachers). Churches may argue that ministry is not a calling to make money; however, pastors, like any other breadwinner, must provide for their families, send children to college, have access to quality medical care, and have access to reliable transportation. Part-time staff pastors may struggle with "donating" time beyond what they are compensated for. Unpaid associate pastors often find themselves without boundaries to structure their time and to prevent burnout. There must be a better way! The good news is that there is.

Structuring a Full-Time Associate's Week

In order to create a healthy and successful working environment for associate pastors, the following model developed by Wayne Oates is strongly recommended.[1] Everyone has seven days in a week. Breaking each day of the week into three sections—morning, afternoon, and night—creates twenty-one sections or blocks of time in which to balance work and personal lives. Each section is roughly four hours. A normal forty-hour work week for most people would consist of ten blocks of four hours. For clergy, a week of full-time pastoral ministry will probably consist of ten to twelve blocks (forty to forty-eight hours), or a maximum of thirteen or fourteen blocks (fifty-two to fifty-six hours).

Because some weeks of ministry are fuller than others, a pastor may have 15 of 21 blocks filled with church-related work (e.g., during Holy Week), but then in the subsequent week he or she should plan to include no more than 9 or 10 blocks of work time. Over the course of an average month, Oates recommends that an average number of about 11.5 blocks be used for each week. Dividing a pastoral work week in this way allows pastors to run errands, socialize with friends, spend time with family, read a book, and exercise. The chart below shows a hypothetical work week for a full-time associate pastor.

Schedule for a Full-Time Associate

	SUN.	MON.	TUES.	WED.	THURS.	FRI.	SAT.
Morning	Sunday school and worship	Office time		Office time	Office time	Sabbath	Men's breakfast
Afternoon		Office time	Visitation	Bible study preparation	Staff meetings	Sabbath	
Night	Leading Bible study		Evening meetings	Church dinner and evening worship		Sabbath	

In reading this chart, a few things should be apparent. First, an associate pastor usually should not work three blocks back to back in one day. There will be one day in a week that is the regular exception—for example, the day that includes a morning Bible study and an evening board meeting. Some churches have such a diversity of weekly activities that an associate could fall too easily into a schedule in which he or she works multiple three-block days. In such contexts, senior pastors and pastor-staff relations committees will need to be intentional about helping the associate to limit ministry commitments to allow only one three-block day a week.

Again, in busy seasons such as Advent or Lent or during the intensive week of Vacation Bible School or revival, pastors may be called to serve in consecutive days of nine to ten hours. And then there are the unforeseen times when community tragedy or multiple funerals create a critical need for pastoral presence—and even associate pastors will find themselves exhausted after emotionally and physically demanding days of pastoral care. These should be exceptions, not the standard expectation, and when such seasons come, be sure to structure flexibility into the preceding or succeeding days—taking the morning off or finishing at noon to balance your work and personal life.

Personal life. That is what the blank blocks in your day or week are for—personal or family time. Preserve a block for a date night with your spouse each week, for your daughter's soccer game, or for helping your son with homework. Use another block to read a book for pleasure or go for a walk or have lunch with a friend. In every week, plan to reserve one day (three consecutive blocks of time) for Sabbath. The human need for Sabbath, a day set apart for rest, applies to all people, both clergy and laity. God sets the example for us in Scripture when, after the six days of creation, the Lord rests. God knows that the human body cannot endure work every day of the week, twelve months of the year. We have limits, and we need rest.

Since pastors, including associates, work on Sundays, their Sabbath may be a Friday or a Monday. Many clergy choose Monday because they want to recover from the demands of Sunday, but some pastors prefer to take Friday off because it gives them a somewhat normal weekend if they take Saturday off as well. Of course, not all pastors are able to take off two consecutive days, not with so many ministry events occurring on Saturdays, but all churches should encourage their pastors to take two whole days off. If a pastor encounters a heavy work week in which he or she works all seven days of the week, at least two days of the following week need to be dedicated to family, friends, and a pastor's personal life.

Finally, a pastor should strive to be at church no more than two or three nights a week. Evenings are usually the only time busy families are home to spend time together. Of course, some weeks demand the pastor's presence at meetings or activities more than other weeks, but as in other busy seasons of the church, be aware of how many of your twenty-one blocks are filled with ministry responsibilities, and balance those with others that are free as soon as possible.

Vacation

If the associate is full-time, most major denominations strongly recommend or require churches to grant pastors, no matter their rank or years of service, four weeks of paid vacation. This ensures that every pastor will be rested, focused, and enriched by time with family. Starting associate ministers off with two weeks of vacation (with additional days or weeks added with time and tenure) is an outdated policy that may result in an associate feeling frustrated, burned out, and underappreciated. There are other ways to reward longevity of service, such as a paid sabbatical every seventh year of service to a church.

If the senior pastor or congregation grumbles that four weeks is overly generous for an associate, provide information that highlights the documented benefits of physical health, job productivity, and vocational satisfaction among workers who are assured of adequate paid time off. Additional studies have compared the condition of the United States work force (which works longer hours and receives less time off) with that of other industrialized nations. In countries such as France or Germany, for example, employers are required to provide at least six weeks of paid vacation in addition to having shorter work weeks.

What about part-time associates? They too should be given time off. Ideally, this should be paid, but even if not paid, this benefit should be written into the associate position. Part-time associates need vacation too. Most likely, an associate is living off another job that does not pay benefits. Since the church is a place of grace and love, offering an associate paid time off would greatly increase that minister's potential for longevity. Two weeks of paid time off and two weeks unpaid is an equitable compensation. If paid time off is not possible, then a church should consider four weeks unpaid leave.

Structuring the Week of the Part-Time Associate

Some part-time associates are not bivocational; they may be retired from their secular career or a previous ministry position. Others are primary caregivers to their children and rely on a spouse's full-time income, which means they balance ministry with substantial parenting and household responsibilities. Some are still students, in which case they juggle church work, school work, and personal life. Then there are associates who are fully bivocational, holding down at least a part-time (if not full-time) job outside their pastoral ministries.

While many part-time associates enjoy flexibility in their schedules, they also have more diverse commitments to balance.

What's more, unlike part-time associates who are retired, primary caregivers, or students, the bivocational associate has accountability to two employers. Both jobs have financial benefits—and economic fallout if responsibilities are not met. It may also be that the associate's secular employment offers far less flexibility in available work hours. It is this reality that compels churches and senior pastors to hammer out a job description or create an assignment list. Having a job description that includes the amount of minimum and maximum pastoral time worked will help associates to balance their lives more effectively. The chart below shows how an associate pastor who works ten to fifteen hours per week could structure that time.

Schedule for a Part-Time Associate

	SUN.	MON.	TUES.	WED.	THURS.	FRI.	SAT.
Morning	Church worship	Secular work	Secular work	Secular work	Secular work	Secular work	Sabbath
Afternoon	Church visitations	Secular work	Church office time	Secular work	Secular work	Secular work	Sabbath
Night				Church office time			Sabbath

Many of the principles that offer best practices for a full-time associate pastor also apply to the part-time associate. These principles include limiting work time (whether church or secular) to two blocks a day, ensuring that no more than one day a week has all three blocks filled with work, allowing only two or three evening commitments each week, and reserving at least one full day as a Sabbath for rest and refreshment. For the associate who is also a student, this portioning of the week will be more challenging when final exams and project or paper deadlines are looming. Still, for a healthy balance of church, secular employment, family, friends, and personal time, experience and experts all recommend a week with eleven to thirteen blocks.

Some part-time associates might find this structuring unrealistic or outright impossible. If so, break the blocks into smaller time spans (two or three hours versus four hours), and do not schedule more than three-quarters of the week for work.

Structuring Time: Urgency versus Emergency

Planning for the urgent and making exceptions for an emergency are two different things. Urgent matters in ministry are important events that do not require immediate action. Emergencies are exactly what the term describes: events that are both important and immediate in their need. A sudden death, a critical accident, an imminent threat to life—these demand prompt pastoral intervention. Evaluating the needs of an individual church member as urgent versus an emergency and having a plan for how to deal with the urgent in a compassionate and respectful manner will facilitate healthy boundaries and aid against clergy burnout. People in a church will have many needs, but the priority of those needs in the life of the associate pastor must be differentiated and weighted.

In fact, one of the blessings of a multi-pastor staff is the ability to provide coverage for one another during vacation or on regular days off. So, the senior pastor who is taking a week away with her family may tell the congregation to contact the associate pastor in her absence. Similarly, on an associate's day off, the congregation may reach out to the senior pastor or another associate. These details may be noted in the church bulletin, disseminated via email, or entrusted to the church secretary or the chair of the board of deacons. With such advance planning, some conflicts between urgent needs and pastoral boundaries may be avoided. But what about the times when planning isn't always possible—or when those plans are overlooked or circumvented by a distraught church member?

For example, the associate who handles pastoral care and counseling is hosting her husband's birthday party on her day off. The house is full of family and friends. The phone rings and she answers, "Hello?" The caller is a long-time church member. "My husband wants a divorce!" the caller cries. The associate is taken aback by the emotional call, and she looks out of the corner of her eye and sees that her husband is about to blow out his birthday candles. The church member yells on the phone, "I need help! What do I do?"

What should this associate do? Should she drop everything for this church member, abandoning the birthday party to rush over to the woman's home? Is this congregant's need an emergency, or it is urgent?

The associate finally answers the caller: "I'm very sorry to hear about this turn of events. I want to talk with you, but I do not think right now would be a good time. It is my day off, and right now, I have a birthday party for my husband and dozens of people here at the house. I want to give you the full attention you deserve. If I tried to meet with you today, I would be distracted knowing that I've left my family and friends on my husband's birthday. I want to be fair to you and to my family. If you need to talk to someone now, the senior pastor is at church, and I am sure she would be more than willing to talk with you. Or, I can make time for you tomorrow."

This is an example of an urgent situation. The pastors at the church rotate their days off to avoid missing pastoral care urgencies or emergencies. The associate was able to give this church member two options: contact the pastor who is on call immediately, or wait and meet with the associate the next day. In this situation, immediate pastoral intervention was not likely to change the circumstances. Marital conflict was most likely present long before this call to the associate was made. Even if infidelity were involved, the events leading up to the transgression (or its discovery) occur over time and the issues require numerous sessions of counseling, which could not be addressed in one hour.

Contrast that illustration with these examples of an emergency need that would require immediate pastoral attention: a church member involved in a serious car accident who has hours to live; a member of the youth group who is on the brink of committing suicide; a wife who calls from her car or a neighbor's home after fleeing an abusive spouse. Situations like these require immediate assistance and emergency action. Depending on the circumstance, it may be possible to keep the caller on the phone while signaling someone else to dial 911 or notify the pastor on call. Other times, the associate may need to drop everything and respond, regardless of who is "off" and who is "on" that day.

Knowing how to respond to every eventuality, crisis, or urgency is difficult, but associates do not have to decide on their own. Quality senior pastors or trusted mentors have gone through the same agony over how to respond to the urgent versus an emergency need. Their wisdom and advice can bring reason and calm to a demanding situation. Deciding as a staff what constitutes an urgent event versus an emergency, having a plan, and supporting other ministers in their decision making will enable associates to navigate difficult decisions. Striving to maintain a healthy sense of self in relation to the work of the associate pastor produces successful pastors and healthy churches.

Daily, Weekly, and Sunday Requirements
of Associate Work
Office Hours and Meetings with Parishioners
Most full-time associates find themselves keeping some sort of regular office schedule. The rhythm of the week requires that calls, emails, and messages be answered promptly in order that

planning and study can take place. While responses to pastoral care emergencies or needs should take precedence, mundane e-mails and other administrative concerns may be considered secondary. Daily interactions with congregants usually require an open-door policy that enables people to stop by to ask a question or chat with an associate pastor. Associates should post their office hours so that the congregation knows they are welcome during those specific times.

It is also helpful to portion one's open-door time so that an associate can set aside segments of time for uninterrupted prayer and study. Don't hesitate to post a message on the door, such as, "Pastor in prayer—Please do not disturb" or "Sermon preparation in progress." Messages like these help parishioners know when a pastor needs some uninterrupted time. The messages also communicate that you take seriously the spiritual practice of prayer or the disciplines of study and meditation.

For associates who may not have an office, it is a good idea to post hours and location or contact information in a central location, such as the church office or bulletin board. You might set up in a conference room or classroom at the church; you can choose a favorite table at a local coffee shop or restaurant. Public libraries may have study rooms available where you could meet with church members, or in warm weather you may identify a public park as a meeting place.

On a cautionary note: it is usually unwise for an associate to meet a congregant in the privacy of your or their home. Choosing a public place or a location that affords a combination of privacy and accountability is safer for pastor and parishioner alike. Home visits are best done when accompanied by a ministry colleague, such as another pastor or lay leader, or when the congregant's spouse or family members are present. Similarly, pastoral counseling sessions should occur at the church office, which offers a more formal and professional environment, and at a time when other church staff are in the building.

Time for Communication and Preparation

Week to week, associates should check in with the ministry leaders under their supervision. Phone calls or even a note asking how their leader's perspective areas are functioning is a helpful weekly activity. Semi-regular office or lunch meetings can accomplish this in a more in-depth fashion. Spending time in prayer, study, and reflection outside an associate's work preparing for ministry-related tasks is also crucial to keep a minister's spiritual life healthy. Weekly or monthly meetings with the senior pastor and staff allow constant communication to flow and minimize conflict. Various duties will differ for each associate pastor depending on their area(s) of focus, but associates should carve out time for preparation, planning, organization, and evaluation of their ministry duties.

Being Visible on Sunday

Associates should allow at least an hour before Sunday morning worship (or the day that worship occurs) and an hour after worship to be available to congregants. Most churchgoers use the primary day of worship at church as the day to make contacts with leaders. The senior pastor may be the one who greets people at the door as worship ends, but associates need to position themselves in high-traffic areas of the church before and after worship. This increased visibility in the church communicates that the associate is open and available for conversation or to meet a ministry need.

This activity requires associates to employ the extroverted side of their personality. Some associates may find this part of ministry exhausting. If engaging the church in gregarious ways is strenuous, more introverted associates may want to read *Introverts in the Church: Finding Our Place in an Extroverted Culture* by Adam S. McHugh. McHugh describes sensible ways in which introverted pastors can serve, minister, and engage a congregation in profound action. Associates should prepare themselves as they enter the church on the prescribed day of worship knowing that their attention is directed toward the people. The goal of weekly worship services should not be to get from the office to the sanctuary (and back again) in the least amount of time. Church members are not interruptions; they are individuals with needs, desires, and cares. A skilled associate knows how to establish conversational boundaries so that no one interaction lasts more than two or three minutes. It is acceptable to say, "I really want to hear more, but I'm on my way into worship. What is a good time for us to meet so that I can give you my undivided attention?" The pathway to and from worship can be fraught with needy people who want to connect with an associate, but wise ministers know that they must treat every interaction with care and compassion.

Working with Committees and Boards

One of the least glamorous jobs of any pastor is attending church board or committee meetings. Senior pastors are usually adapted to plugging into church meetings, but associates may not have all the right tools to make a meeting run smoothly. Understanding the purpose, vision, and goals of each ministry board or committee is immensely helpful in making the most of the time spent in meetings. Effective meetings are everyone's desire in the secular and church world, but few are able to master meetings. Meetings are inextricably linked to church work, but few seminaries or educational instititions offer courses in how to run meetings. The following suggestions are ways that associates can make the most of attending or leading meetings.

Take Quality Notes

Quality note taking on the essential facts, places, people, and ideas will give an associate an impressive reputation for meeting memory. Do not get caught up in recording minutiae. Transcribing details of a twenty-minute discussion on the children's parable will bog down your note taking. Just write down phrases or words that strike you as important to the discussion. Be sure to record any decisions that are made, any actions that are approved or assigned, and the dates and times for related events or future meetings.

Be on Time
Starting and ending a meeting on time will encourage your committee members to come back. Create incentive for others to get to the meeting on time. Being habitually late to meetings will give the impression that your life is disorderly. Who wants to waste time waiting? Or worse, the committee might have to waste time to bring you or others up to speed on what has happened in the meeting.

Stick to the Agenda
People will mentally check out of a meeting after about an hour. Have an agenda and stick to it. Have a stated beginning and end. If a longer meeting is scheduled, plan to take a break midway through. This will encourage the committee members to stay focused. If there is not enough time for a topic, table it until you can give it due attention in the next meeting.

Stop Engaging Discussions That Go Nowhere
"Who headed up Vacation Bible School last year? Chris? Remember the time when . . . ?" Conversations like these happen innocently in meetings. Congregations process people, places, and events through memory and story. It is healthy to think about the good times or the bad times in order to gain perspective about a future ministry. However, do not waste twenty-five minutes talking about Chris's exploits. If board

members want to reminisce, politely ask them to save that for after the meeting.

Use Technology When Possible
Why meet when an email or Survey Monkey can poll a committee on a topic? Use technology whenever possible to circulate meeting minutes, give consent on the agenda, or share ideas. Digital storage websites, video conferencing, and online meeting software can allow committee members to meet remotely. Technology can never replace a face-to-face meeting, but it can enable committees to better use their time.

Speak Your Mind (with Reservation)
As an associate, if you hear something that piques your interest or concerns you, please say something! Do not be a passive presence in a meeting; as a leader in the church, you have something to add. If you hear a committee member criticize the senior pastor or another congregant, gently remind that committee member to speak with love and grace about others in the church. If an idea is presented that is problematic, do not immediately quash it. Ask open-ended questions—questions that require more than a yes or no answer. Let the discussion encourage the presenter to think through the idea and present it again after he or she has worked on it some more.

Remember, You Are a Pastor Too
Make sure the meeting opens in prayer—and return to prayer if an important decision needs to be made. Share a devotion, meditation, or Scripture that can encourage the group in its work. If you hear a pastoral care concern, act on it. Do not wait for the senior pastor to become involved, but do communicate the concern or need to the senior pastor. Encourage the committee in its work and let each person know her or his time is valuable.

Associate pastors are called to minister to people, even if that person is not in your ministry focus area.

Do Not Dominate, and Do Not Let Others Dominate
You may be a chair or ex-officio member of a board, but that does not mean you are allowed to dominate the discussion. Next time you are in a meeting, record how much time you spend talking. Do you make more statements or ask more questions? Be honest in your self-assessment. If you see another person controlling the discussion, ask those who are silent in the meeting what they think. Some people need to be invited before they will volunteer an opinion.

Be a Sounding Board
The senior pastor may not be able to attend every meeting, but you can go in his or her place. People may want to convey ideas or suggestions for ministry that you can pass on to the senior pastor. Also, associates can help committees refine their ideas before approaching the senior pastor with an idea.

A Concluding Word
Being a team player means that you, as an associate, can bring leadership to the areas with which you come in contact. Having a well-balanced life, a structured work week, and the ability to guide committees toward efficiency can give associates an advantage in ministry. Associates who do not need constant hand holding in the way they manage their responsibilities and challenges will encourage the senior pastor to give an associate new and exciting opportunities in the ministry of the church.

Associate pastor ministry can be a lonely place, but it does not have to be so. Being an associate colleague to a senior pastor should not be an experience where you are seen as an "underling." Putting the ideas, best practices, and suggestions in this book can change the way churches, staffs, and senior pastors view and treat the associate pastor. The goal of this book is to encourage associates to see themselves as fully fledged ministers who are critical to church leadership. Providing associate pastors with this identity in the church can help them understand their role in relation to the senior and can help clarify an associate's role in the mission of the church. Truly, a team needs many members with different gifts. A team, with a good senior pastor as leader, can be allowed to excel in its specialty without micromanagement or excessive interference. The senior pastor can give guidance and encourage the associates as team members in their work, but ultimately associate pastors must be given a chance to discover their limits, strengths, weaknesses, and victories.

Discussion Questions for Churches

1. How well do you think your associates structure their work week? What areas could they improve?

2. What can the church and the senior pastor do to support a healthy balance of an associate's personal life and ministry?

3. How does the pastoral staff handle who is on call? What system is in place for the church to have pastoral care coverage while a pastor is on a day off?

4. How much time does the associate spend doing ministry work? Is it too much or too little? What could be done to change this reality?

5. What expectation does the church have for associates to be present at evening functions, meetings, or events? Is this a healthy or unhealthy expectation?

6. How can the church encourage an associate pastor to maintain mental and physical well-being?

Discussion Questions for Associates

1. What do you find is the most challenging aspect of planning your work week?

2. What system do you have in place to balance church demands and family?

3. How many nights do you spend at church? If it is consistently more than three, how can you make changes to your schedule to limit your nights out?

4. What day is your Sabbath? How do you spend the day? How do you recharge for your ministry?

5. How often do you find yourself sacrificing too much of your personal time for urgent demands of the church? How do you determine urgency from emergency?

NOTES

1. Wayne E. Oates, *The Minister's Own Mental Health* (Great Neck, NY: Channel, 1961).

How to Plan for an Associate Pastor

Planning to hire an associate takes many months. The timeline here is a guide to bringing a new associate on board in your church, and it applies mainly to free-church traditions, which typically use a search-and-call process. Churches that do not use this process may use this timeline in a different manner depending on which denominational leader makes decisions for pastoral placement.

Two Years before Hire
■ Clarify the need for an associate.
■ Will the associate be part-time or full-time?
■ What is the vision of the associate's work?
■ Form a search committee or use the church's pastor-staff relations team, along with the senior pastor, to survey congregants about their expectations of an associate pastor.
■ Ask the congregation to dream of future ministries. What are areas of growth or areas that need to grow? Can an associate pastor help those areas?

Eighteen Months before Hire
■ Create a job description.
■ In what areas will the associate minister?
■ What resources will you give the associate pastor to succeed in his or her job?

■ How will you compensate the associate? If the associate will be full-time, how does his or her compensation compare with that of the senior pastor? If the associate will be part-time, how will the church compensate her or him?

Sixteen to Four Months before Hire
■ Search for associates and collect résumés.
■ Have the search committee choose the most desirable candidates by using specific criteria, as deemed appropriate by the search committee or church.
■ Hold phone interviews with the top four to six candidates.
■ Schedule face-to-face meetings with one to three of the strongest candidates.

Four Months to One Month before Hire
■ Decide on one or two final candidate(s).
■ Finalize compensation.

Two Months to One Month before Hire
■ Offer a paid visit for the candidate(s) to visit the church.
■ Make the necessary preparations for the candidate (and the family) to visit the church and preach a sermon.
■ Begin the polity-specific process to formally approve the candidate for associate ministry.

Sample Job Descriptions

Following are two representative job descriptions, one for a full-time associate pastor and the other for a part-time associate.

Full-time Youth and Family Associate Pastor

A qualified candidate must possess a master's degree in divinity or equivalent with a strong background in working with young people. The candidate will:

■ be able to lead traditional and contemporary worship.
■ be an active preacher and share in pulpit responsibilities (six to eight times a year).
■ conduct appropriate baptisms, weddings, and funerals.
■ support the doctrinal beliefs or statements of faith of the congregation.
■ exhibit enthusiasm for Christian formation in young people.
■ be proficient in Bible study.
■ able to work with a committee made up of adult volunteers.
■ establish a family activities committee and plan extensive programs for children and their families.
■ work with young adults between the ages of eighteen and thirty and engage them in the ministries of the church.
■ possess the organizational skills to plan large functions such as retreats for fifty to sixty people, mission trips, youth trips, and other events.

- establish small-group ministries and training for their leaders.
- offer counseling for youth, young adults, and families.
- work with the director of education in planning and presenting educational classes and seminars.
- be an enthusiastic and cooperative member of the ministerial and professional team.
- work well with the senior pastor.
- be active in laity groups and in the community.

Part-time Education Associate Pastor (20 hours per week)
A candidate should have a relevant degree or training in education with specific focus on adults. The candidate will be expected to:

- articulate and communicate a clear, compelling vision and strategy for education ministries.
- evaluate, select, and use curriculum that embodies the mission and vision of the church.
- establish annual and long-range goals for education ministries that are consistent with the church's mission and vision.
- expand, create, encourage, execute, and assess the church's education program for children and adults.
- work with the church's weekly preschool program to ensure goals are met.
- work in concert with the church staff and senior pastor.
- enlist, train, direct, organize, and congratulate teachers, staff, and volunteers in the educational ministry.
- be present Sunday mornings for Sunday school coordination.
- assist in leading worship and preach four to five times a year.

APPENDIX C

Case Study: Transition from Volunteers to Paid Staff

Town Congregational Church is a large suburban church with several pastors and staff members. The church has strong programs for children, youth, and adults. For a number of years, directors had been hired to run the children's programs. Recently, the church has relied on volunteers and other church staff to run its children's ministry. Parents expressed frustration about how the church was handling the children's ministry. At the last church business meeting, the church voted that all children's programs will be fully coordinated by paid and experienced children's ministers. David was hired about four months ago as the part-time associate pastor for children's ministries. He is responsible for directing and coordinating the children's Sunday school programs, children's Wednesday night programs, and Vacation Bible School (VBS).

Six months before VBS started, David begins to talk with Susan, who was the volunteer coordinator for VBS last year. David wants to get an idea of how many children attended last year, how much was spent, who taught the children, who helped with crafts, who helped with music, what types of games were played, and other things related to VBS. Susan is very helpful and gives David a good idea of the type of program that has been run in the past.

Five months before VBS starts, David begins to ask teachers and workers who were involved in the past if they would be interested in doing similar jobs again this year. Most volunteers want to return and serve as teachers, run games, help with music, and supervise crafts. Prior to David's hire, Town Congregational Church used Church Ink materials for VBS. Parents have told the committee that their children loved the program. The Children's Committee has decided to use that curriculum again. David is given the curriculum and makes a form used in the church bulletin asking for more volunteers to help with VBS. Many more church members volunteer to help. David receives all of the materials from Susan that were used last year for the publicity so that he can understand how the program was presented last year. Susan even emails David last year's registration spreadsheet so that the church can use it again. David thanks Susan for helping with the upcoming VBS program. David sends out a mailing to all families announcing the dates, times, and theme of VBS and how to register their children.

About four months before VBS, David starts to receive some odd questions regarding VBS and Susan's role. A church member asks David, "Why is Susan not being allowed to be involved in Vacation Bible School?" David is confused because Susan has been so helpful and has never asked or expressed interest in being involved in VBS.

That same day, David receives an email from Susan. Susan has also sent the email to the pastor. In the email, Susan describes how David has refused to allow her to be involved with VBS and how David has stolen all of her ideas about VBS. Susan also describes how she was prepared to handle VBS and how she even bought the upcoming VBS director's handbook with her own money. The email also states that the church does not treat its members right. Susan threatens to leave the church and withdraw her offering each month if the situation is not rectified. What makes matters worse is that more church members are asking David why Susan cannot be involved with VBS. Some church members are even asking David what he did to provoke such a reaction from Susan. Still other church members who have heard what is happening tell David that this is not the first time Susan has created an uproar.

Stop and Reflect
After reading the email, David is called into the senior pastor's office. David is new on staff and doesn't want church members to get the impression that he is difficult to work with. If you were David, what would you do? How would you respond to church members' questions regarding Susan?

APPENDIX D

When to Stay, When to Leave

There comes a time in every associate's ministry when the question arises, "Should I start looking for another position?" Since the average associate pastor stays three years at any given church, transition to a new ministry occurs frequently. The following questionnaire provides an associate with a way to assess if it is time to stay in the current ministry setting or time to leave.

(T or F) I feel appreciated, welcomed, and affirmed.

(T or F) My senior pastor gives me freedom to explore new ministry ideas.

(T or F) I look forward to coming to church.

(T or F) I regularly find opportunities to fail or succeed.

(T or F) My senior pastor is a great mentor.

(T or F) My church supports my work and publicly affirms my gifts in ministry.

(T or F) I feel that my job evaluations are accurate and help me to be a better minister.

(T or F) The senior pastor trusts my judgment.

(T or F) Conflicts among the church staff occur infrequently.

(T or F) Most of the time I am not micromanaged.

(T or F) My input is valued by the church leaders and appreciated in meetings.

(T or F) The senior pastor and I have a good relationship.

(T or F) I am asked to preach more than twice a year.

(T or F) I can see myself staying in my current church
two more years.
(T or F) I feel that I can speak my mind in confidential
staff meetings.
(T or F) I do not feel burned out by my work at church.
(T or F) I look forward to bringing new ideas to the
senior pastor or church leaders.

To calculate your score, count how many times you answered
false. Then see the list below.

0–3   You are golden! You should stick around and
grow your ministry.
4–6   You enjoy your work and most likely can stay
(with some reservations).
7–9   You feel that your work is important, but it might
be time to pray, revaluate your ministry, and
consider a future move.
10–13   You struggle to find value in your current
ministry setting. Start strengthening your
résumé because it is most likely time to find a
new position.
14–17   This is not working out for you. It is time to go.

For the minister who is trying to discern the right (or wrong) time
for transition in ministry, I highly recommend *When the Spirit
Moves: A Guide for Ministers in Transition* by Riley Walker and
Marcia Patton (Judson Press, 2011).

Compensation

Generally, a full-time associate pastor can be compensated at a rate of 70 to 85 percent of the base pay for the senior pastor. In the example below, the associate pastor's pay is calculated at 80 percent of the senior pastor's pay. Differences in the 80-percent ratio are noted.

	Senior Pastor	Associate Pastor
Salary*	$60, 000	$48,000
Housing or parsonage value*	$15,000	$12,000
Retirement life insurance	$9,600	$7,580
Travel reimbursement	$2,000	$1,600
Reimbursement for books	$800	$640
Reimbursement for conferences	$1000	$800
Medical insurance	covered in full	covered in full
Vacation**	4 weeks	4 weeks

*Some churches allow their pastors to split their salary and house as needed. For example, if the total salary and housing package for a pastor is $50,000, then the pastor could split that number into separate housing and salary numbers as allowed by federal law.
**As noted previously, most major denominations recommend or require that all pastors receive four weeks of paid vacation.

Part-time associate pastors can use this chart as well. For example, a full-time pastor might make $48,000 a year; a part-time associate (20 weeks) who does similar work and lives in the same area would make $24,000 in base pay.

BIBLIOGRAPHY

Bowen, Murray. *Family Therapy in Clinical Practice*. Northvale, NJ: Jason Aronson, 1978.

Byassee, Jason. "Team Players: What Do Associate Pastors Want?" *Christian Century* 123, no. 2 (2006): 18–22.

Hoge, Dean R., and Jacqueline E. Wenger. *Pastors in Transition: Why Clergy Leave Local Church Ministry*. Grand Rapids: Eerdmans, 2005.

McHaugh, Adam S. *Introverts in the Church: Finding Our Place in an Extroverted Culture*. Downers Grove, IL: InterVarsity Press, 2009.

McIntosh, Gary L., and Samuel D. Rima Sr. *Overcoming the Dark Side of Leadership*. Grand Rapids: BakerBooks, 2001.

Nouwen, Henri. *In the Name of Jesus: Reflections on Christian Leadership*. London: Darton, Longman and Todd, 1989.

Oates, Wayne E. *The Minister's Own Mental Health*. Great Neck, NY: Channel, 1961.

Oden, Thomas C. *Pastoral Theology: Essentials for Ministry*. New York: HarperCollins, 1983.

Peterson, Eugene. *The Contemplative Pastor.* Grand Rapids: Eerdmans, 1989.

Rathbun, Russell. *nuChristian.* Valley Forge, PA: Judson Press, 2009.

Thumma, Scott, Dave Travis, and Warren Bird. "Mega Churches Today 2005." Hartford Institute for Religion Research and Leadership Network, 2005.

Walker, Riley, and Marcia Patton. *When the Spirit Moves: A Guide for Ministers in Transition.* Valley Forge, PA: Judson Press, 2011.

Willimon, William. *Pastor: The Theology and Practice of Ordained Ministry.* Nashville: Abingdon, 2002.